Thomas Bewick
Graphic Worlds

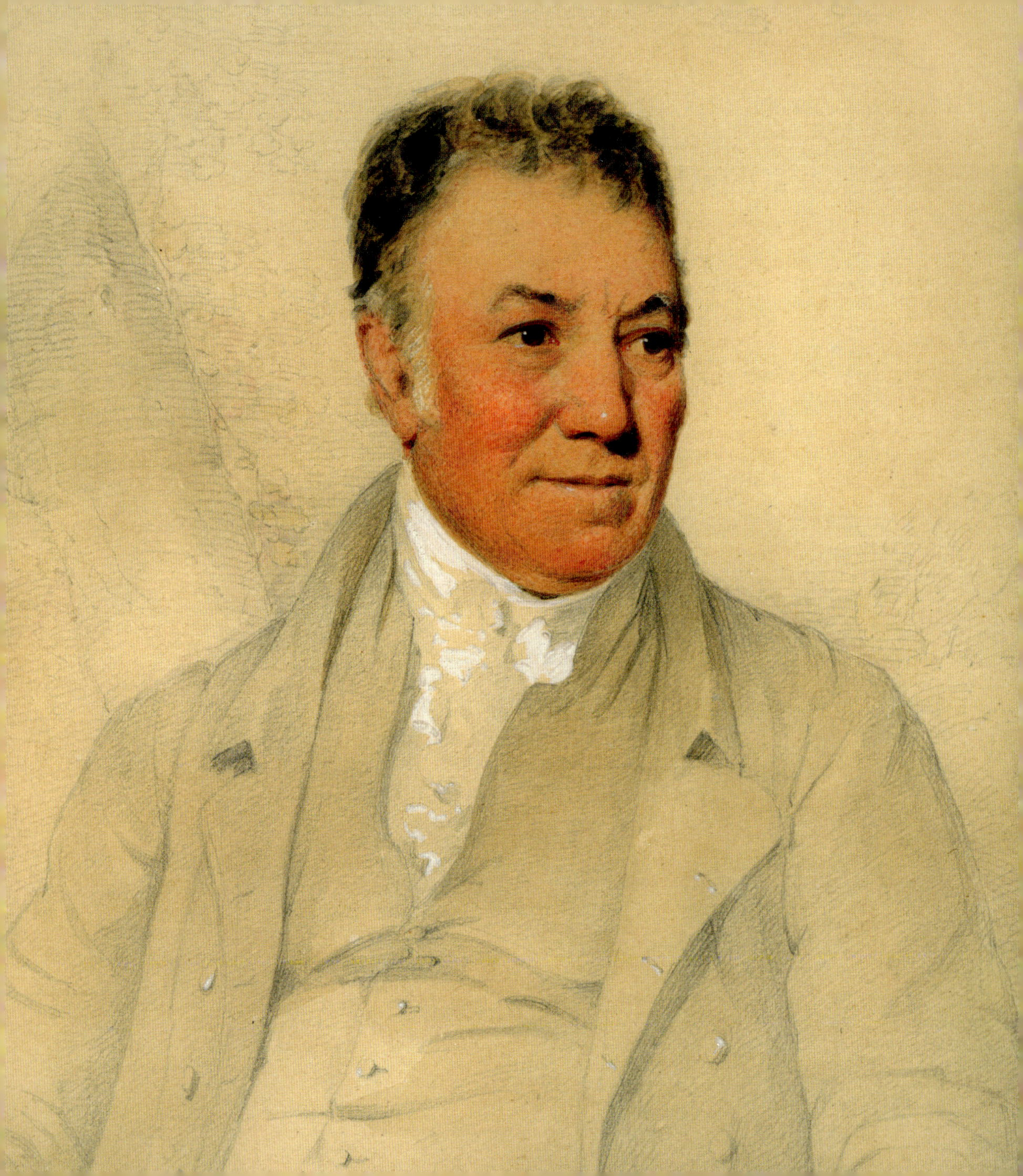

Thomas Bewick
Graphic Worlds

Nigel Tattersfield

The British Museum

A la memoria de Alicia Cristina Ojeda
A media luz los besos,
A media luz los dos …

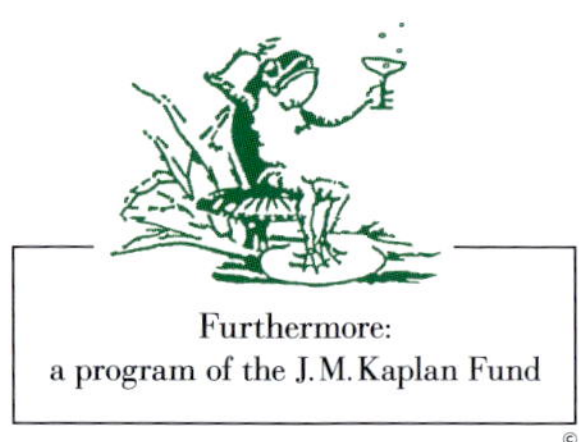

This publication has been supported by Furthermore: a programme of the J. M. Kaplan Fund.

First published in 2014 by The British Museum Press
A division of The British Museum Company Ltd
38 Russell Square, London WC1B 3QQ
britishmuseum.org/publishing

Nigel Howard Tattersfield has asserted the right to be identified as the author of this work.

A catalogue record for this book is available from the British Library
ISBN: 978-0-7141-2691-3

Designed by Jade Design
Printed in China by 1010 Printing International Ltd

Frontispiece: Thomas Bewick, aged 60, by William Nicholson, July 1814.
Detail from a watercolour on paper. Natural History Society of Northumbria.

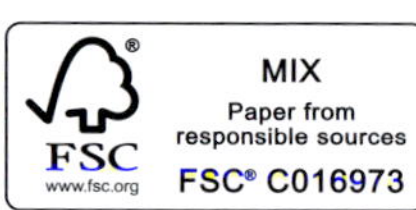

Contents

Introduction

When William Wordsworth wrote enviously in his *Lyric Ballads* of 1800, a few years after Thomas Bewick's *History of British Birds* first saw the light of day, 'Oh now that the genius of Bewick were mine / And the skill which he learn'd on the banks of the Tyne', he crystallized the notion, current ever since, of Thomas Bewick as an unlettered genius, communing with Nature, remote from the tawdry world of commerce. Though it makes for fine poetry, nothing could have been further from the truth.

Thomas Bewick came up the hard way. A tough (but in many ways enviable) childhood was followed by seven years hard graft as an apprentice in an engraver's shop in Newcastle upon Tyne, one of the busiest, sootiest towns in the kingdom. After a brief sojourn in London (which he disdained), Bewick returned to the selfsame workshop and remained there all his days, first as a partner with his erstwhile master Ralph Beilby, from 1799 as sole proprietor and finally with his son Robert as a partner from 1812. This workshop was his life, from the year he joined as a fourteen-year-old apprentice in 1767 until his death in 1828. It also provided the profitable bedrock of commercial engraving, which facilitated the creation of Bewick's three acknowledged masterpieces, the *General History of Quadrupeds* (1790), the *History of British Birds* (1797 and 1804) and the *Fables of Aesop* (1818). Masterpieces they may have been, but they were never allowed to interrupt commercial work, the daily bread of the jobbing engraver. Fortunately for us, Bewick's eldest and most devoted daughters, Jane and Isabella, having lived far beyond their allotted span and seeking a national stage upon which to display their father's graphic talents, presented much of his considerable output to the British Museum in the early 1880s, a fraction of which has been employed to illustrate the present volume (see page 140).

Although we regard the present age as one of rampant consumerism, the latter half of the eighteenth century would have given us a run for our money. A rise in disposable income amongst the rapidly expanding 'middling' classes together with a vast increase in the quantity of manufactured goods and novelty items available at affordable prices (thanks to the application of steam and other power sources to the manufacturing process) created an unprecedented spiral of consumption. There was yet another significant shift, largely brought about by the improvements to the road system instigated by the Turnpike Acts, which originated in the late seventeenth century. These were intended to facilitate the flow of goods and services around the country. However, an unexpected consequence was the gradual demise of the open-air trading fairs and local markets, and a decrease in the numbers of previously ubiquitous pedlars and hawkers touting their ribbons, trinkets and slipsongs deep into the countryside. This was mirrored by the rise of the fixed warehouse, a house for wares; in short, a shop. Here goods could be securely stored and displayed and customers welcomed in permanent, comfortably appointed surroundings by managers who cared deeply for their reputations.

As we understand it today, shopping was largely unknown until the latter half of the eighteenth century and the creation of the verb 'to shop' dates from the 1760s. By this time, shops as purely retail establishments did exist but most had a manufacturing facility attached to them. In 1800, Thomas Bewick's workshop would have been typical: a shop front to the street with a counter where business was transacted, rooms above where engraving was executed and (in his case) a printing office at the back. England was rapidly becoming – as the Scottish economist Adam Smith had noted by the 1790s – a 'nation of shopkeepers', to such an extent that by the latter half of the eighteenth century there were more shops per head of the population than in the opening decade of the twenty-first century.

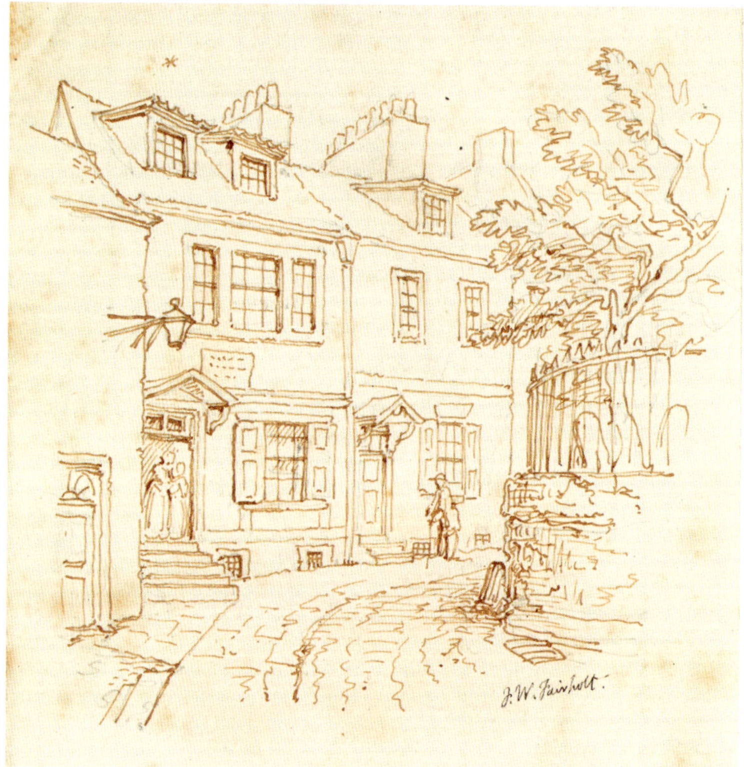

View of the Bewick workshop in St Nicholas Churchyard, Newcastle. Pen and ink drawing by Frederick W. Fairholt, dated 19 October 1854. The firm of Beilby and Bewick moved here in 1790 and the shop was occupied by Robert Bewick until 1849. 178 × 110 mm. Private collection.

Unlike the peripatetic retailers who had preceded them, the new generation of eighteenth-century shopkeepers required much in the way of stationery: order books, trade cards, invoice headings, billheads and so forth. Image and branding, commensurate with the aspirations of the shopkeeper, became a matter of importance, to be reflected in the typography and decoration displayed upon whatever piece of paper pertained to the business. This was largely the province of the engraver.

By a similar token, proprietors of manufacturing workshops, busily turning out metal goods such as snuff boxes, hairpieces, buckles, watch cases, buttons, sugar tongs and suchlike, the staple of a thousand workshops in London, Birmingham, Manchester, Sheffield, Newcastle upon Tyne and elsewhere, recognized the desirability of being able to offer their customers the option of personalized decoration. This sometimes took the form of enamelling but more frequently it was the engraver who was called upon to embellish the item with initialled ciphers, crests, or rococo swags, scrolls and flourishes. In many cases, this was a form of security engraving for light-fingered domestic staff were a problem, even in the homes of relatively modest tradesmen.

Whereas in London each part of the engraving business had its specialists – writing engravers for lettering, bright engravers for decorative motifs on metal, map engravers, clock-face engravers, bottle-mould engravers, to name but a few – provincial or country engraving workshops were expected to provide craftsmen who could take all these divisions of labour in their stride and still turn out a decent job. The workshop established in 1765 by the young Ralph Beilby in Newcastle was typical, a one-man operation which catered for a local audience. This was no artist's atelier, merely an unpretentious attempt by an entrepreneurial engraver of limited skills to profit from the growing demand for every branch of engraving: on gold, silver, ivory, brass, copper, pinchbeck and even upon the humblest material of all, wood. All such work was grist to his mill, for he 'refused nothing, coarse or fine'.

*　　*　　*

The workshop (and the material culture which it served) was Ralph Beilby's natural habitat. His father had been a highly regarded Durham jeweller and watchmaker, gold and silversmith whose production ranged from marrow scoops to coffee pots before he fell on hard times. His mother's family were also

Durham gold and silversmiths, so Ralph and his three brothers
were steeped from birth in the ethos of the luxury-goods trade.
The eldest surviving brother, Richard, learned seal engraving
in Birmingham, and took up silversmithing on his return to
Newcastle. William also departed for Birmingham where he was
apprenticed to a drawing master and enameller, applying the
technique to wine glasses and ceremonial goblets after he returned
home. Ralph had practised as a jeweller and seal engraver,
probably with his father. Thomas, the youngest, commenced in
business as a drawing master, and later became a dealer in luxury
metal goods in Birmingham. The brothers had been outstanding
scholars at Durham School and were proficient in the classics and
French, and in addition Ralph was a fine musician. They kept
horses, were habitually courteous, lived prudent, God-fearing lives
and exhibited all the attributes of genteel tradesmen, if not of
the gentlemen they aspired to be. In many ways they were typical
representatives of the emerging 'middling' classes, who made up
nearly a quarter of the population by the 1780s.

The same could not be said of Thomas Bewick. His family
were hard working and respectable, but genteel they were not.
His father, a capable, plain-speaking man, held the lease on an
eight-acre smallholding called Cherryburn on the north-facing,
wind-scoured south bank of the Tyne, a dozen miles upriver from
Newcastle. Whether this small farm ever produced any revenue
is doubtful; Bewick's family numbered nine in all and whatever
the farm produced would have been largely consumed on site.
At least the costs of heating the farmhouse and cooking for the
family were slight as Bewick's father also held the lease on a small
landsale colliery which lay further up the slope, on Mickley Bank.
Managing both smallholding and pit was hard work, and the young
Thomas Bewick, as the eldest child, was expected to play his part.

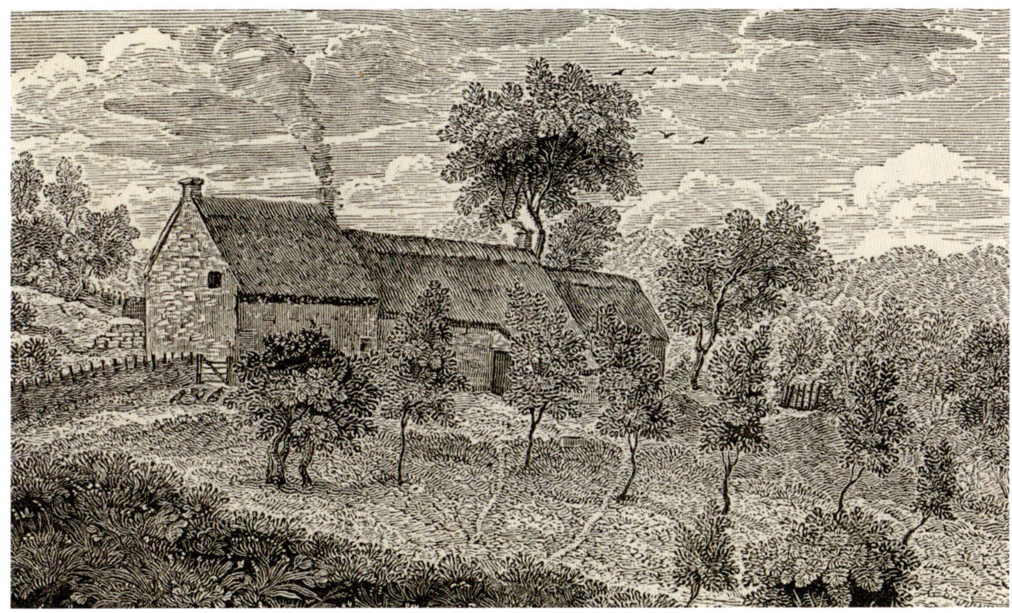

Cherryburn, the birthplace and childhood home of Thomas Bewick, engraved on wood by him after a drawing by his brother John. The farmstead remained in the possession of the Bewick family until the early years of the 20th century and is now a National Trust property incorporating a museum devoted to Bewick's life and work. 75 × 118 mm. Private collection.

From the age of six his everyday tasks consisted of mucking out the cow byres, foraging for animal feed during deep midwinter, shepherding his father's flock, managing the horse working the winding gear at the pithead and even plying his pickaxe at the coalface.

By the age of eight or so, Bewick was a formidable, unbiddable child, as much a trial to his parents and schoolmasters as they were to him, and his existence, as he later admitted, 'a life of warfare'. When playing truant and when not at the beck and call of his father, he ran free and unfettered across the expanse of Mickley Common, making mischief for miles around. Yet despite all the acts of derring-do, his was a sensitive soul. He may have been exposed to little in the way of traditional book-learning but he had gained an empiric understanding of nature, of the changing seasons and even of right and wrong. Most importantly, he was beginning to make his mark on his immediate world. This he

achieved by means of chalk upon flagstones or roughly cut quill
pens dipped in bramble juice upon scraps of paper or board. If
a surface would support an image, it was his canvas. This passion
for 'figuring', as Bewick called it at the time, never having heard of
the word 'drawing', brought him the acclaim of his neighbours. It
was a habit that persisted all his life; his workshop account books
display occasional marginalia, as do many of his letters.

When the question arose of Bewick's apprenticeship,
his parents, though 'greatly at a loss as to what to fix upon',
acknowledged that his future lay in the field of artistic endeavour.
As luck would have it, his godparents both had connections
with Newcastle's artist-craftsman community. His godfather was
Thomas Blackett, the husband of his aunt Sarah. He was a gold
and silversmith and foreman to John Langlands, Newcastle's most
prominent goldsmith. Much of Langlands' output of silverware
– serving spoons, ladles, castors, cream jugs, salvers, teapots and
so forth – was already being decorated and embellished by Ralph
Beilby. His godmother, Mrs Simon of nearby Bywell St Peters

Informal invitation to lunch
from Bewick to William
Kitchen, a mapmaker and
engraver, 19 December
1786. Drawing in pen
and ink with autograph
inscription, 60 × 195 mm.
Private collection.

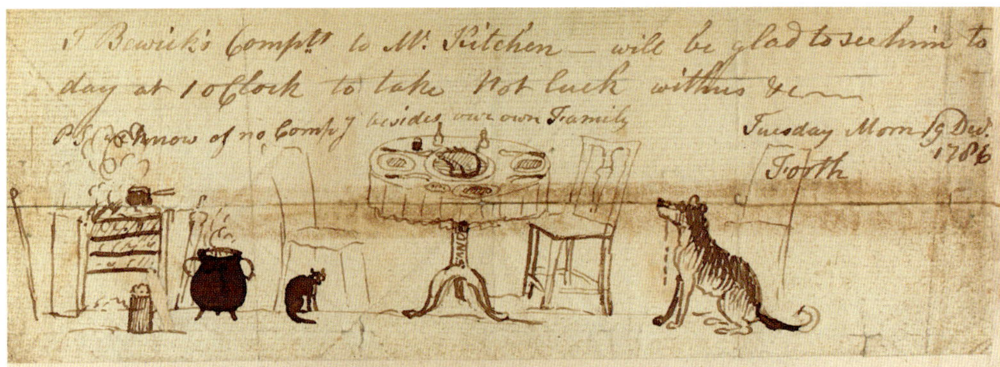

(where Bewick's father and grandfather had both farmed in years
gone by), was the wife of the vicar and numbered William and
Ralph Beilby amongst her closest friends. She was aware that
each brother was looking for a likely lad to serve as an apprentice
and she may have also known that Thomas Bewick had inherited,
through the generosity of his grandmother, the sum of £20, held
in trust for his apprenticeship fee. One weekend the two brothers,
probably in response to representations by both godparents, rode
out to Cherryburn where they took tea with Bewick's parents and
Mrs Simon. The promise evident in this roughly spoken, uncouth
but not uncivil lad must have been plain to the Beilbys; each offered
him an apprenticeship. Bewick declined William's overtures, 'liking
the look & deportment of Ralph the best'. Upon such insignificant
prejudices history sometimes turns.

*   *   *

The die was cast. In October 1767, although his heart was 'like
to break', Bewick bid farewell to Mickley Common and all
his childhood haunts and, perched behind his father, rode to
Newcastle. As was the practice of the day, Bewick initially lodged
with the Beilbys, for an apprentice was expected to imitate not
only the skill of his master but his mindset as well. The young lad
was kept upon a tight rein. At work, customers had to be treated
politely, their requests respected, their foibles indulged. At home,
the hierarchy within the Beilby household ranked Bewick on a par
with the servants, another cross to bear.

Unlike anything he had ever known, the workshop was a world
of artifice. All manner of engraving on metal flooded in. During
the first week of his apprenticeship Bewick watched Ralph Beilby
engrave arms on two steel seals, crests on six tablespoons, a mustard

pot and matching spoon, a name on a whip, an invoice heading
and two plates for a tea chest. The highpoint of the following
week was the engraving on copper of a £1 note for a local bank.
Bewick learned quickly and proved an industrious apprentice,
ready to turn his hand to anything and rapidly rivalling his master.
With little apparent effort, he assimilated the evolving tastes and
fashions of the day at the same time as he absorbed the technical
demands inherent to his craft. At first, Beilby gave him the hard,
unrewarding jobs, keeping the finer work for himself. This proved
a blessing in disguise; one of the materials for which Beilby (as the
son of a goldsmith) had no sympathy, was wood. Entirely natural,
not precious, not fashionable, not manufactured, not wrought, not
profitable and employed only in a printing press for its illustrative
qualities (which decorated mere chapbooks or lowly cottage
literature) Bewick, unhampered by any of the conventions and
prejudices which hindered his master, made it his own. Within a
few years, Bewick had skill enough to handle fine work on precious
metals too. Just as importantly, his honesty was beyond question;
in the early autumn of 1770 Beilby handed over to his seventeen-
year-old apprentice and departed for six weeks in London. The
experiment was obviously successful. During the summer of 1774,
Beilby absented himself for three months in the capital, ostensibly
to master new techniques of engraving on copper, leaving the
whole of the workshop under Bewick's management.

By now Bewick had left the Beilby family and set up in
lodgings, initially with his recently widowed aunt Sarah Blackett,
and then with Ned Hatfield, proprietor of a lodging house much
frequented by other apprentices and journeymen craftsmen.
They in turn introduced Bewick to a host of 'tradesmen of the
genteel sort', drapers, saddlers, hardwaremen, china dealers,
brush-makers, potters, printers, engine-makers and rope-makers

amongst them. Being of lively and enquiring dispositions, they met at 'Constitutional' and 'Philosophical' societies, bringing him the friendship of even more tradesmen and an unceasing flow of orders for invoice headings, trade cards and receipts.

By 1778, following an unhappy eight months in London and his accepting Ralph Beilby's offer of a partnership, Bewick was responsible for most of what would be termed today the 'creative output' of the workshop, which now also numbered a small group of apprentices. In consequence, Bewick set the style both graphically and typographically for the commercial interests on Tyneside. Beilby remained on hand to execute the coats of arms and crests which so delighted him, but he was a diminishing force in the workshop being also engaged in watch-glass manufacture, watch- and clock-making tools (called 'Lancashire tools' by the trade), enamelled clock faces and watchmaking. His attempt to set up a button manufactory (buttons, like buckles, were high-fashion items) in the workshop was firmly rebuffed by Bewick, who had more than enough on his plate. The workshop was overwhelmed, a victim of its own success. Gold and silversmiths commissioned endless initials and crests and bright-engraved decorations on their wares, hardwaremen requested floral swags on trinket boxes, jewellers wanted fine lettering and posies on rings, saddlers wanted crests on whip handles and ciphers on saddle nails, sword-makers required decoration on hilts, gun-makers their names on lockplates and powder flasks, undertakers the names of the dearly departed on coffin plates, printers came calling for children's book illustrations, newspaper editors fancied a change of masthead, travelling showmen needed to blow their own trumpets with illustrated handbills. The list was endless for the universe of trades and businesses was expanding relentlessly and 'the furious Itch of Novelty' showed no signs of abating.

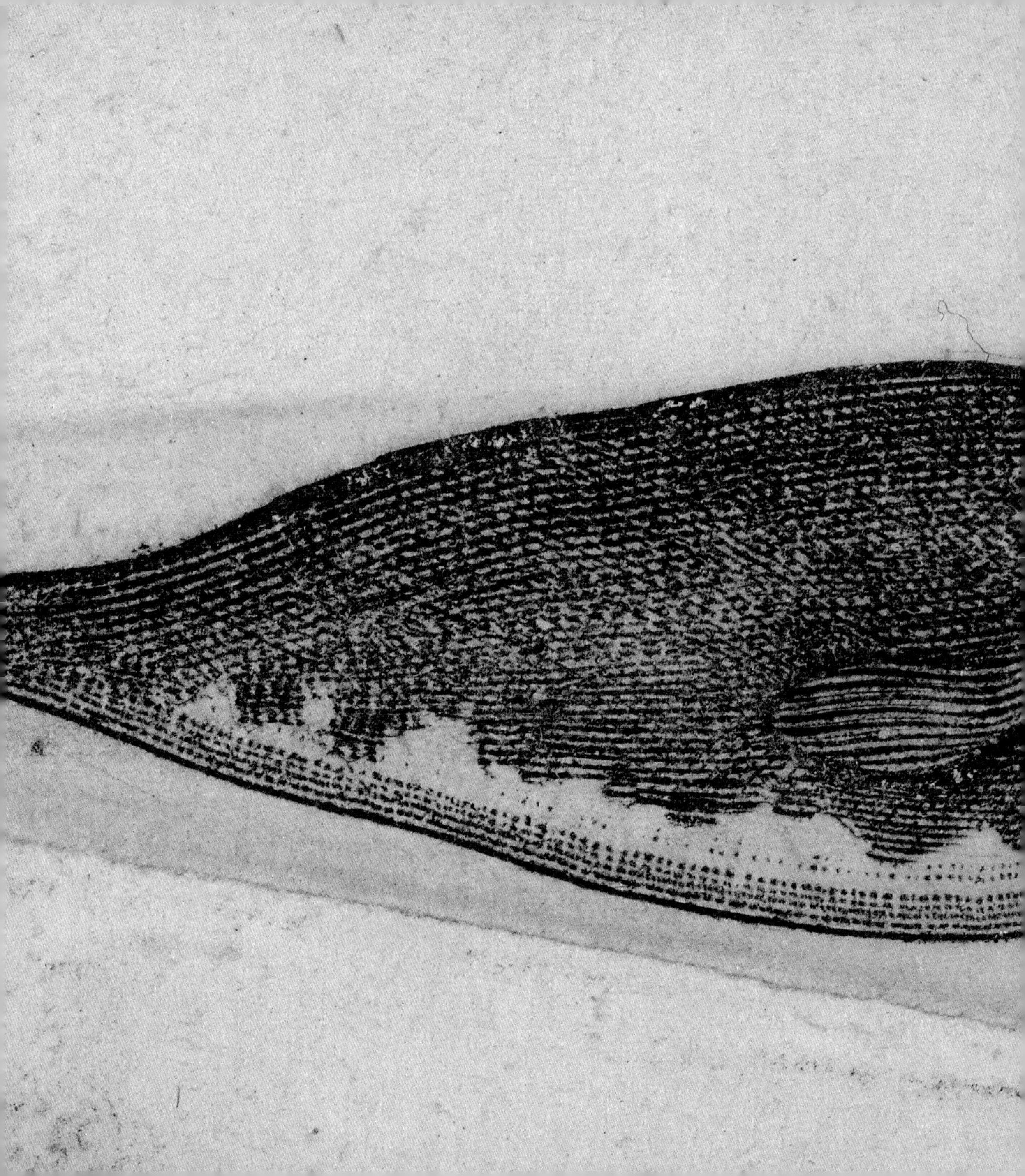

The World of
Decoration

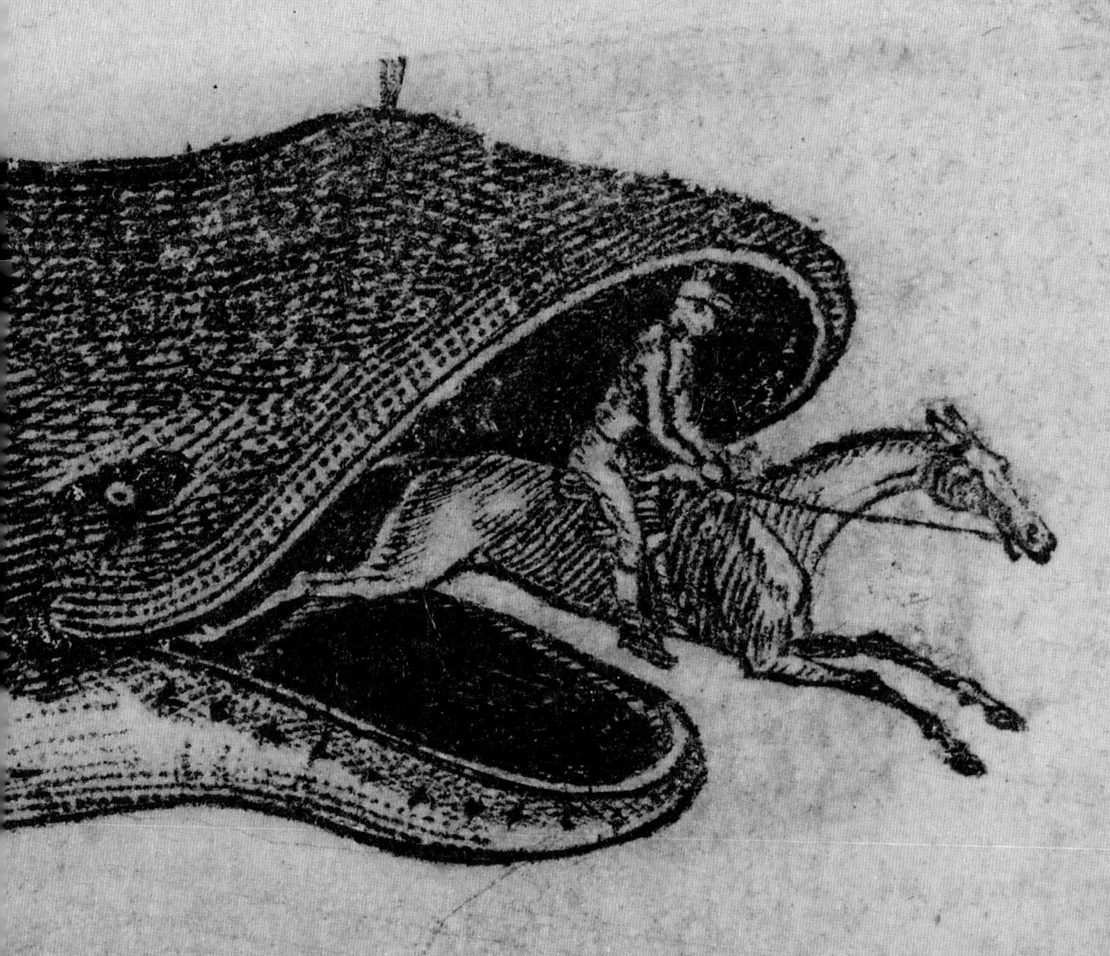

Silver

Silver suited the 'prudent luxury' to which the 'middling' classes
and minor gentry aspired, and quickly found itself upon their tables
 as the fashion moved away from pewter and earthenware, and
silver – like glass and china – became increasingly affordable. Silver
did not possess the cachet of gold but neither did it embody notions
of extravagance. It could justifiably be regarded as a potential
heirloom, an investment and as a husbanding of financial resources.
Though God forbid it should ever come to this, it could conceivably
be sold in times of hardship. It was the perfect metal for an Age of
Reason, gleamed reassuringly in candlelight, reflected pleasantly in
glassware, and lent a sense of occasion to minor domestic rituals.

Domesticity ruled, almost literally. The accession of George III
to the throne in 1760 ushered in a thrifty monarch with a strong
sense of family values who prized hearth and home above all else,
and whose influence percolated down through the different levels
of society. As the opportunities to socialize outside the home
increased with coffee houses, pleasure gardens, routs and assemblies,
so the idea of the home as an ordered, harmonious and welcoming
refuge became paramount. Domestic rituals which had previously
been restricted to the wealthy – the taking of tea, the drinking of
chocolate, for example – were now emulated by the 'middling'
classes. A precipitate fall in the cost of imported commodities meant
that tea, sugar, chocolate and coffee were regarded by 1800 not as
luxuries but as commodities of mass consumption.

Coincidentally, a new code of politeness and self-respect
(civility) affected these rituals; visiting, taking tea and dining all
 incorporated ceremonial aspects which were punctiliously
observed. For example, visitors were to be welcomed with the 'best'
tea service (which pleased the chinaware retailers) and the 'best'
silver teapot demanded attendance by the paraphernalia of
gentility – matching milk jug, cream boat, tea strainer, teaspoons,

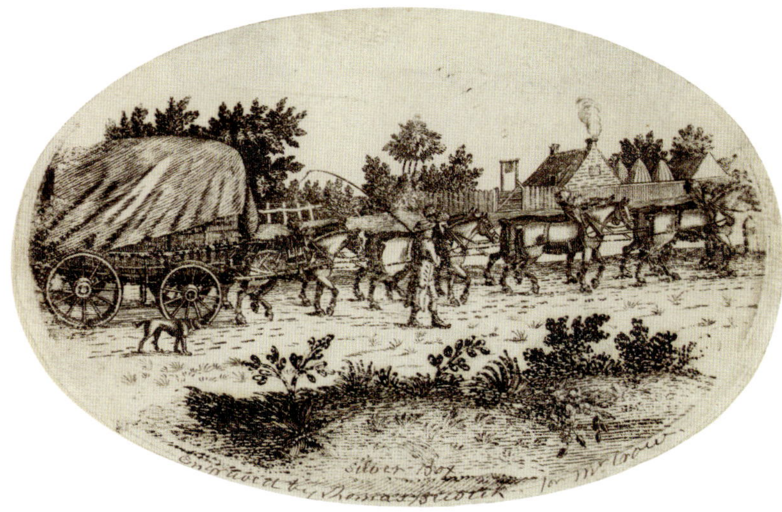

sugar tongs and sugar bowl. Dining, even on a modest scale, required silver tableware which went far beyond cutlery (for soup, fish, meat, pudding, fruit and cheese) and encompassed marrow scoops, sauce boats, pepper castors, salt dishes, ladles and a panoply of salvers, tureens and serving dishes.

Silver was also the metal of choice for official occasions, for celebrations, presentations, awards and rewards. It played its part in church services, adorned hunting jackets and was fashioned into racing trophies. When fashion changed, or the object was damaged beyond repair, or it became irrelevant in its current form, it was melted down. Thomas Bewick caused a few impressions of engravings from silver to be taken on paper, probably as an aide-memoire, but few other visual records remain of the vast procession of silverware that passed through the workshop for engraving.

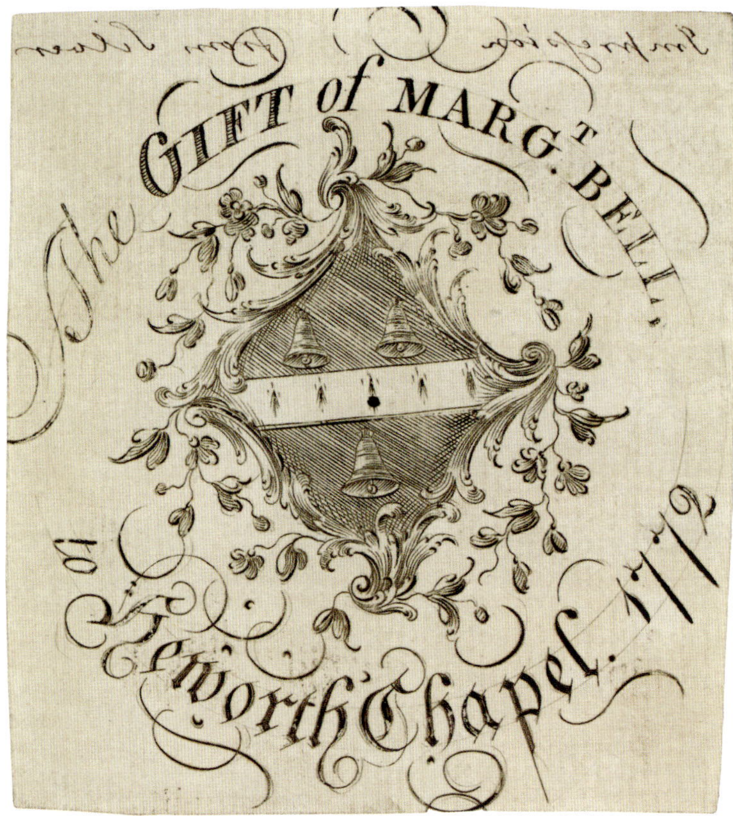

Arms and inscription engraved by Ralph Beilby, 3 March 1773, at a charge of 7s. 6d., on a chalice made by James Crawford of Newcastle. It shows Beilby's graphic strengths in lettering and armorial engraving. Impression on paper, 82 × 73 mm. (Reversed from the original impression on paper, which carries the inscription by Jane Bewick, 'Impression from Silver'.) British Museum 1882,0311.3160.

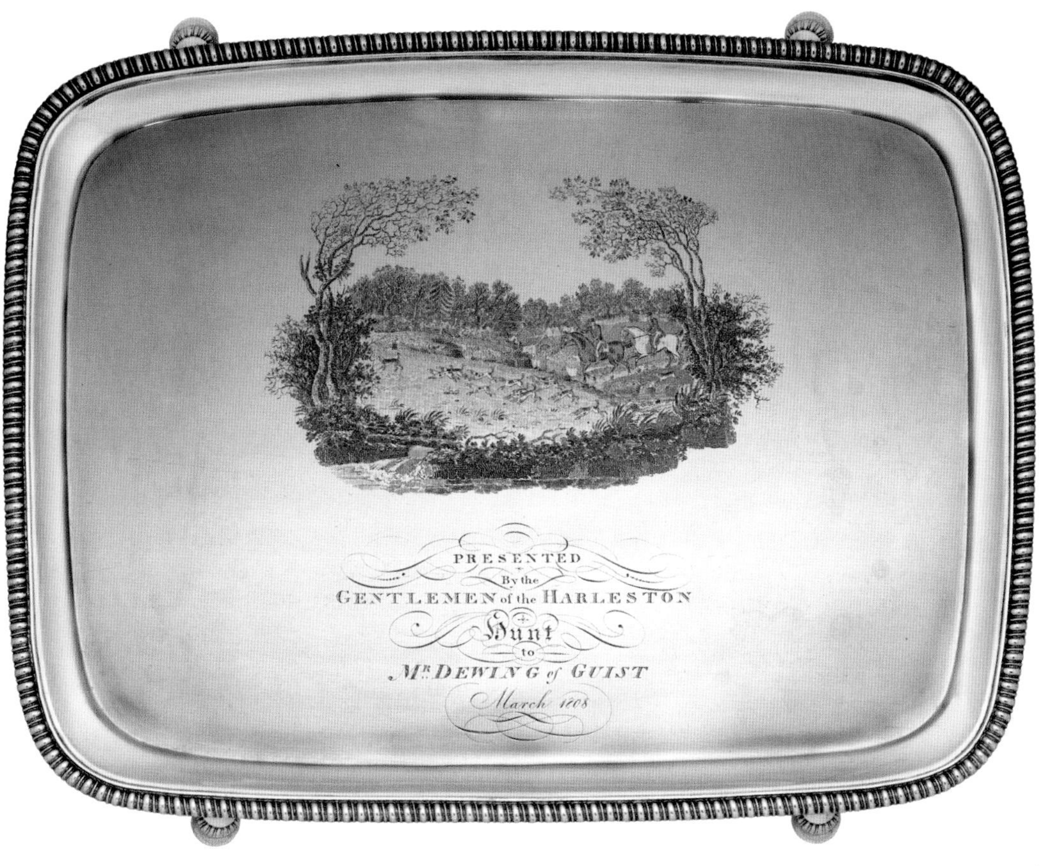

Harleston Hunt salver made by Ann Robertson, Newcastle. Engraved by Thomas Bewick, 22 August 1808, at a charge of £3 13s. 6d. The salver was presented by the members of the Harleston Hunt to Edward Dewing, a wealthy landowner of Guist in Norfolk, in acknowledgement of his gift of a pack of hounds. In 1827 Dewing died of an apoplectic fit whilst out hunting. Engraving on silver, size of salver 378 × 290 mm. © Victoria and Albert Museum, London.

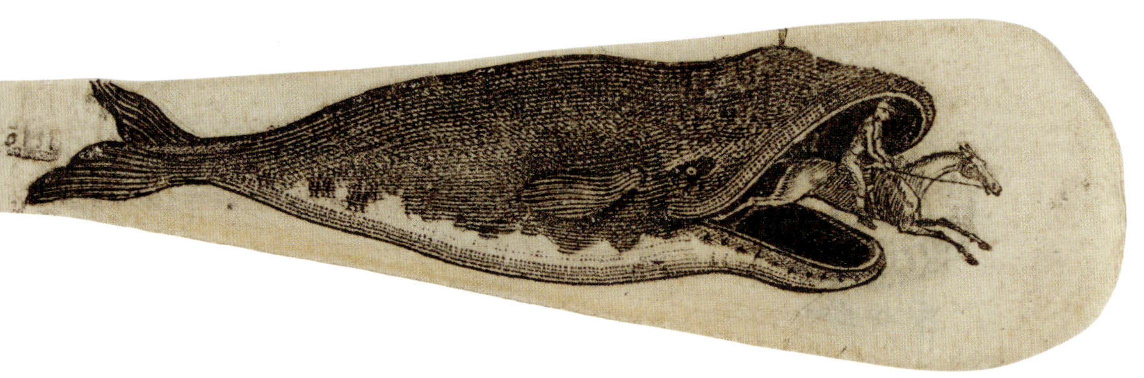

Device for twelve fork handles, engraved 1 March 1800 at a charge of 2s. 6d. each for George Baker, landowner and banker of Elemore Hall, Co. Durham, regarded as one of the finest amateur horsemen of his day and who delighted in hunting and cockfighting. Impression on paper, 22 × 66 mm. British Museum 1882,0311.3167.

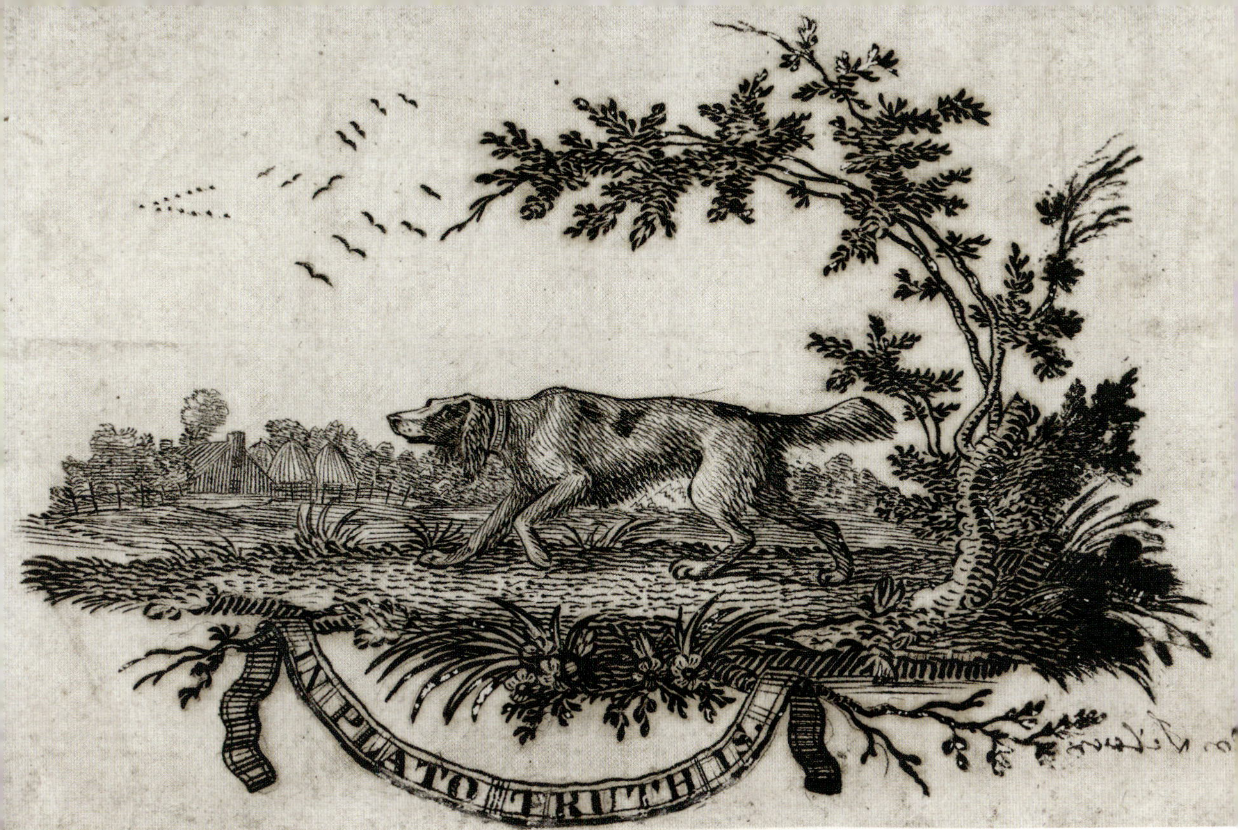

Device for a wine tray(?), *c*. 1778, probably celebrating a favourite dog. The motto beneath the setter 'In Plato Truth is', is an echo of the Latin tag 'In vino veritas', and is a knowing reference to Plato's aphorism, 'A dog has the soul of a philosopher'. Impression on paper, 60 × 93 mm. (Reversed from the original impression on paper.) British Museum 1882,0311.3169.

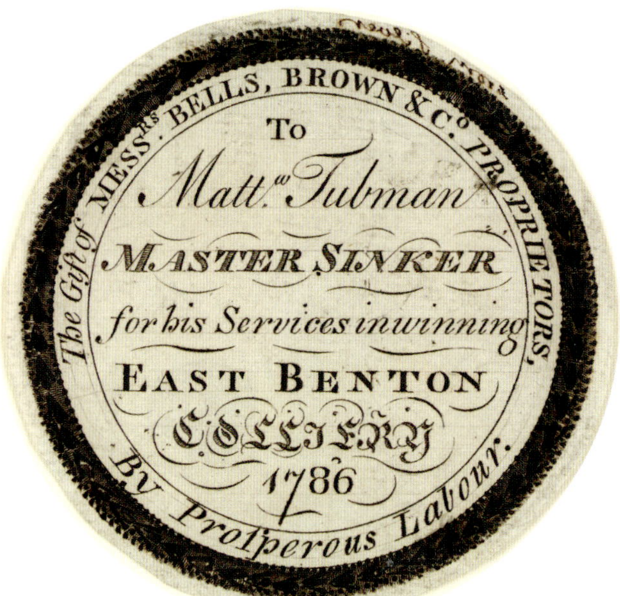

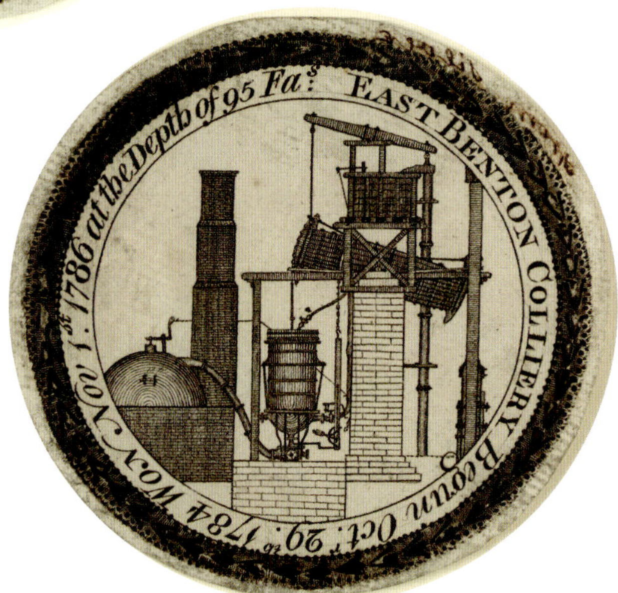

Commemorative medal (one of four) made by Langlands and Robertson, engraved (front and back) by Thomas Bewick, 5 December 1788, at a charge of 11s. 6d. each; this example was awarded to Matthew Tubman, master sinker (shaft engineer) at East Benton Colliery. Impression on paper, 68 mm (diameter). (Both images reversed from the original impressions on paper.) British Museum 1882,0311.3163; 1882,0311.3165.

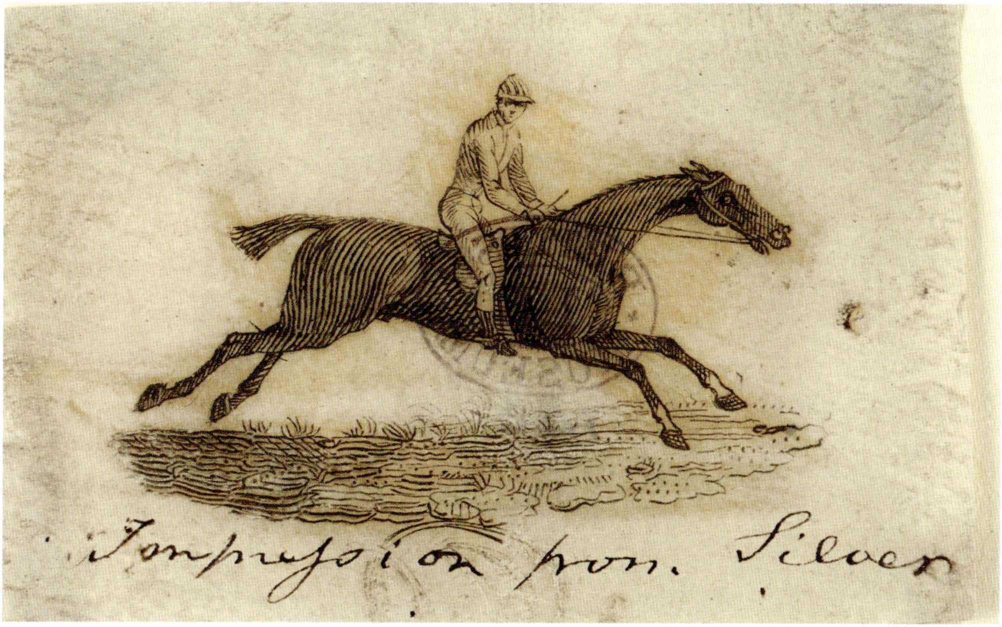

Racehorse device for a cup, commissioned by Ann Robertson, silversmith, engraved 6 November 1802, at a charge of 6s. 0d. Impression on paper, 32 × 52 mm. British Museum 1882,0311.3171.

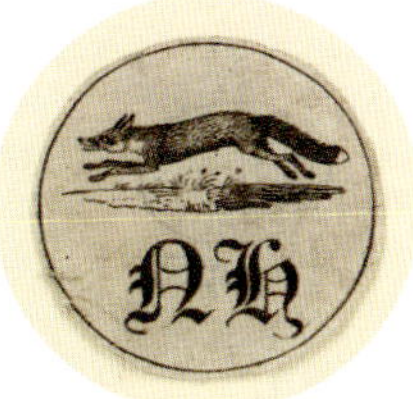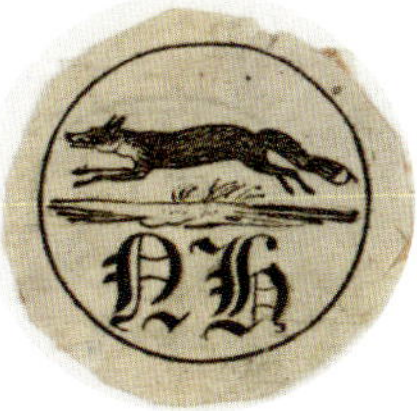

Netherwitton Hunt devices, probably commissioned by silversmiths Pinkney and Scott, engraved 22 September 1781 upon 16 jacket buttons at a charge of 6d each. Impression on paper, 23 mm (diameter). (Reversed from the original impressions on paper.) British Museum 1882,0311.3172; 1882,0311.3786.

Ceramics

For everyday domestic situations which did not demand silver, or for more modest households, ceramic tableware or crockery sufficed. It did not possess the cachet of silver but was an acceptable and widespread alternative. Tea, coffee and chocolate pots, with their attendant milk jugs and other paraphernalia formed much of the output of the pottery manufactories that lined both banks of the Tyne (and contributed so fulsomely to its polluted state). Virtually everything that could be made of silver (cutlery apart) could be created in a pottery, from dainty cream boats to pierced 'wicker' baskets.

As was the case with silver and glass, the manufacturers of ceramics were drawn to Tyneside in the latter half of the eighteenth century by the plentiful local supply of cheap coal for firing their kilns. The presence nearby of substantial deposits of brown clay and flint quarries in County Durham helped sustain the industry. White clay and fine-quality potter's clay were not available locally, but formed the return cargo (as ballast) taken up by Newcastle colliers after delivering coal to London, part of the continuous flow of bilateral trade between Newcastle and the capital.

Tyneside and Wearside potteries, though rarely capable of producing goods that could stand comparison with those of Wedgwood or Spode, nonetheless attempted to emulate them. However, the bulk of their output remained traditional crockery, much of it of great charm, and some of it decorated with views of local sights such as the cast-iron Sunderland Bridge or illustrations of popular ballads such as *The Vicar and Moses*.

These decorative elements were applied from transfer prints. A copper plate was engraved or etched and an impression on thin paper taken off on the pottery's own rolling press and straightaway dabbed on by hand, inky side down, to the unglazed bisque surface of the bowl or plate, jug or tankard, which quickly absorbed the design. The paper was eased away and discarded and the object fired and glazed, fixing the decoration.

Over the years, the workshop of Ralph Beilby and Thomas Bewick numbered upwards of twenty local potteries amongst its customers. The first commission was for 'a Flower Plate for an earthenware manufactory', which Beilby recorded engraving in May 1768. This was followed by a host of 'borders' and 'sprigs', 'hunting scenes', 'Nankin Patterns' (Chinese patterns transfer-printed in blue), and 'Classical Subjects in Outline for Vases', the latter in 1817 and 1818. This commission, from the local pottery of Sewell and Donkin, probably reflected public interest following the Lord Mayor of Newcastle re-equipping the Mansion House with Spode's 'Greek Pattern' tableware a few years earlier.

These designs were rarely, if ever, signed by Beilby or Bewick and their workshop's contribution to Newcastle and Sunderland pottery remains largely unappreciated. The ephemeral nature of the paper impressions means that only a handful have survived, but they show Bewick successfully transferring his skills from wood engraving to etching on copper and bringing the lively touches typical of his graphic art to a hitherto unfamiliar medium. Unlike silver, a prestige material demanding a more restrained approach, pottery allowed him to relax and display his own brand of homespun humour.

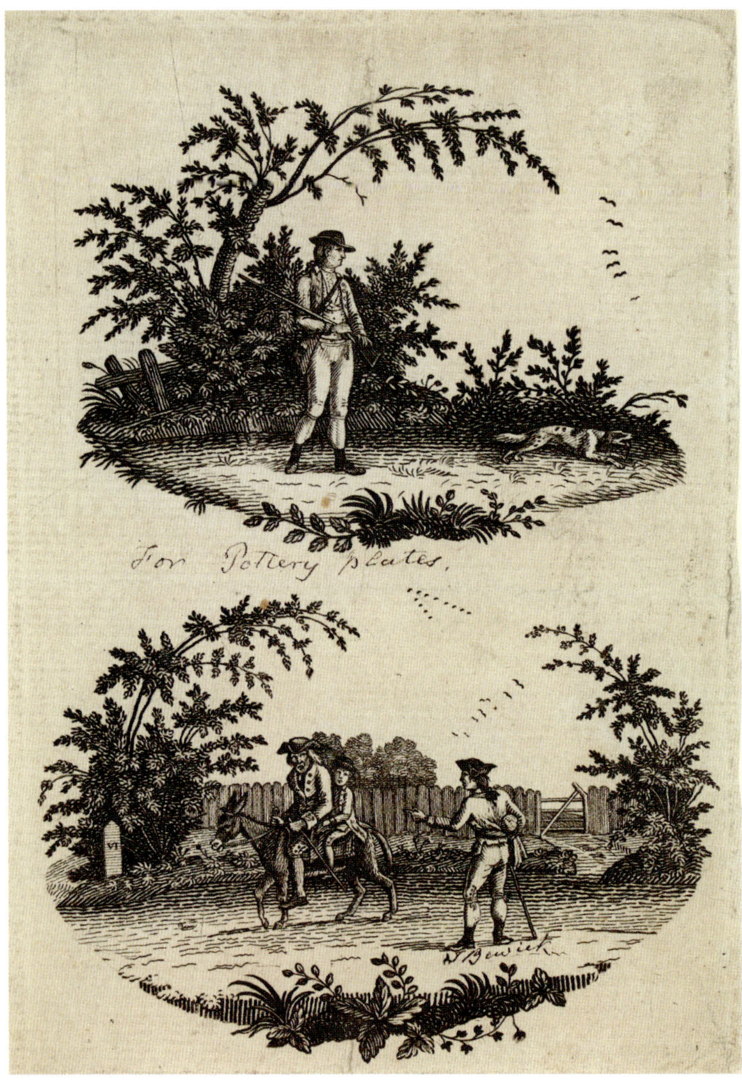

A pair of rural scenes
commissioned by
Christopher and John
Maling of the Hylton
Pottery in May and June
1788, designed and
etched by Bewick at a
charge of 15s each. Both
scenes are inspired by
Bewick's own woodcuts
for the *Select Fables* of
1784. The upper image is
reminiscent of 'The Snipe
Shooter', whilst the lower
is directly copied from
'The Miller, his Son and
their Ass'. Jane Bewick's
later inscription 'For
Pottery plates' should be
interpreted as '[copper]
plates for a pottery'.
Impressions on paper,
printed as a pair,
125 × 92 mm. British
Museum 1882,0311.3175.

Themes of rural idylls and rustic lovers were a well-established convention on pottery tea canisters, cups, saucers and bowls by the 1760s. These two designs date from the mid-1780s and may correspond to the commissions for two 'landscape plates' for quart pots from James King of St Anthony's Pottery, designed and etched by Bewick in June and July 1785 and charged at £1 5s. 0d. each. They illustrate 'The Contrast', a wry view of the married state, showing the heady days of courtship and the less heady days that follow as the new wife catches her idle husband enjoying a quiet whiff. Impressions on paper, each 90 × 110 mm. British Museum 1882,0311.3174; 1882,0311.3173.

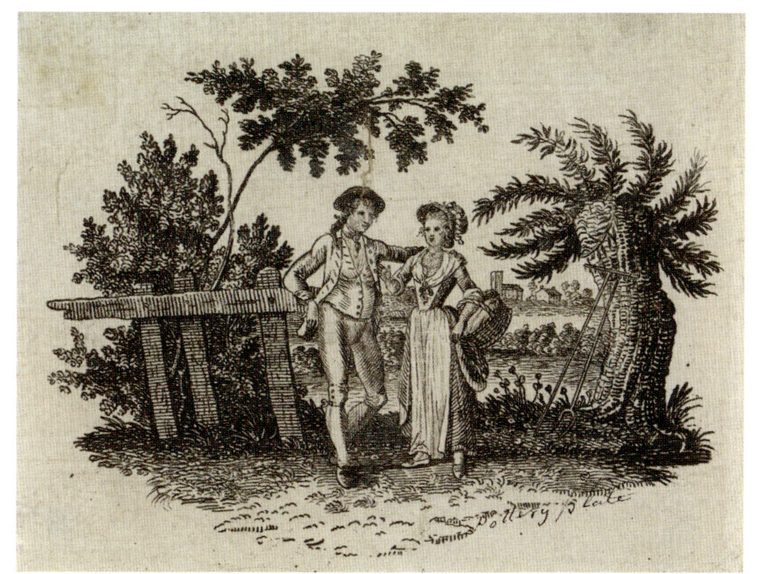

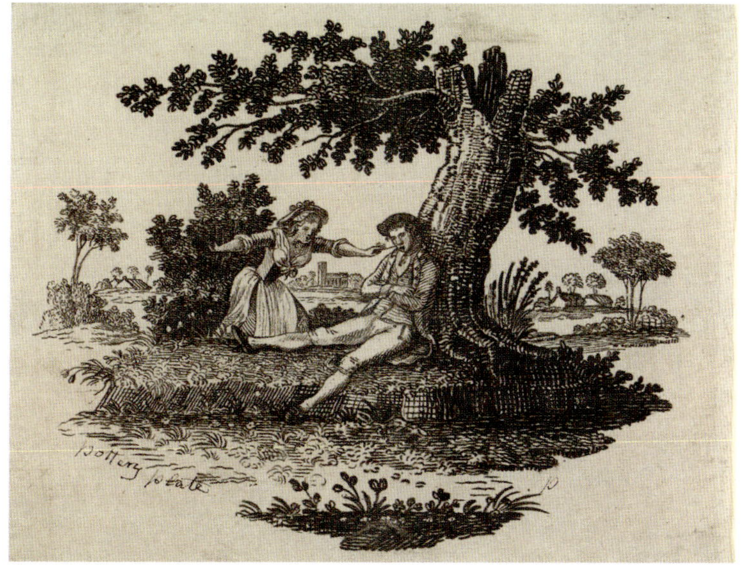

Decorative device for a lobster plate commissioned
by the Newcastle banker and industrial magnate Isaac
Cookson junior for his personal use, designed and
etched by Robert Bewick, 15 June 1816, at a charge of
£2 12s. 6d. Impressions occur printed in black, blue and
bistre-red. Impression on paper, 115 × 210 mm.
Courtesy of the Natural History Society of Northumbria,
Great North Museum: Hancock.

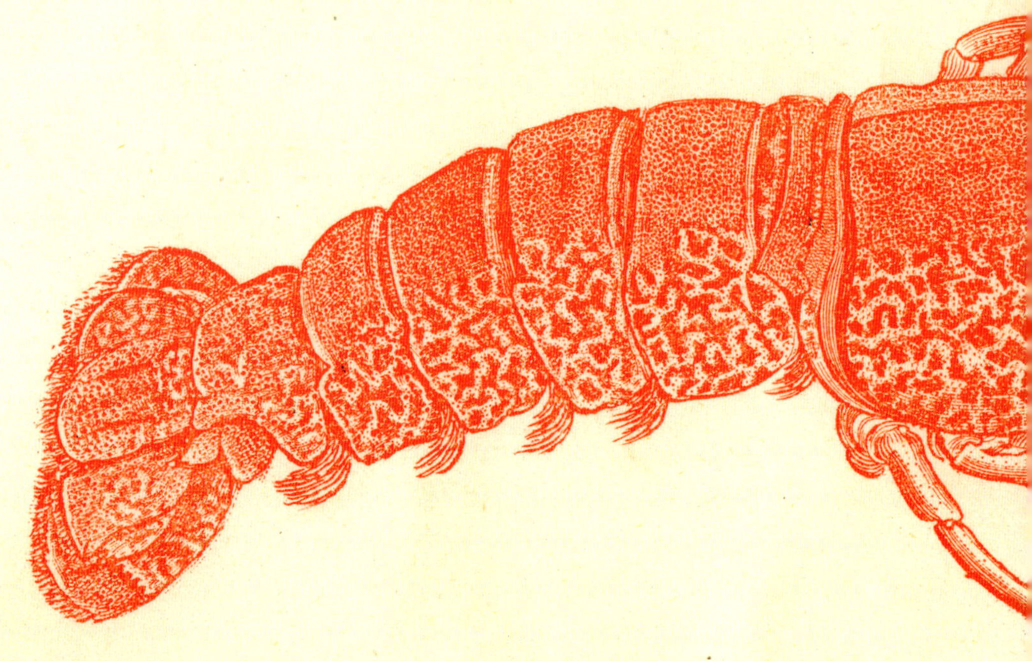

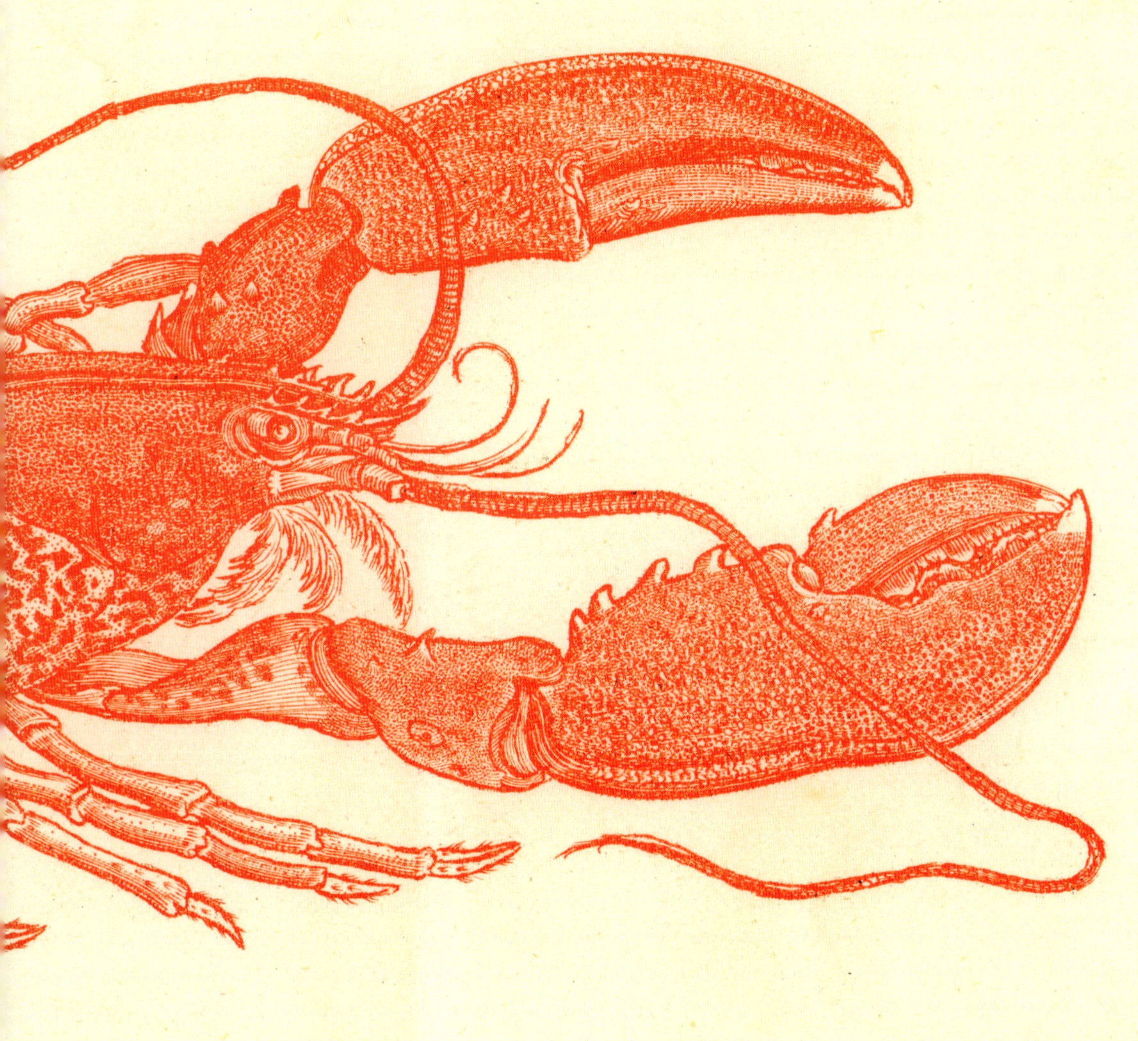

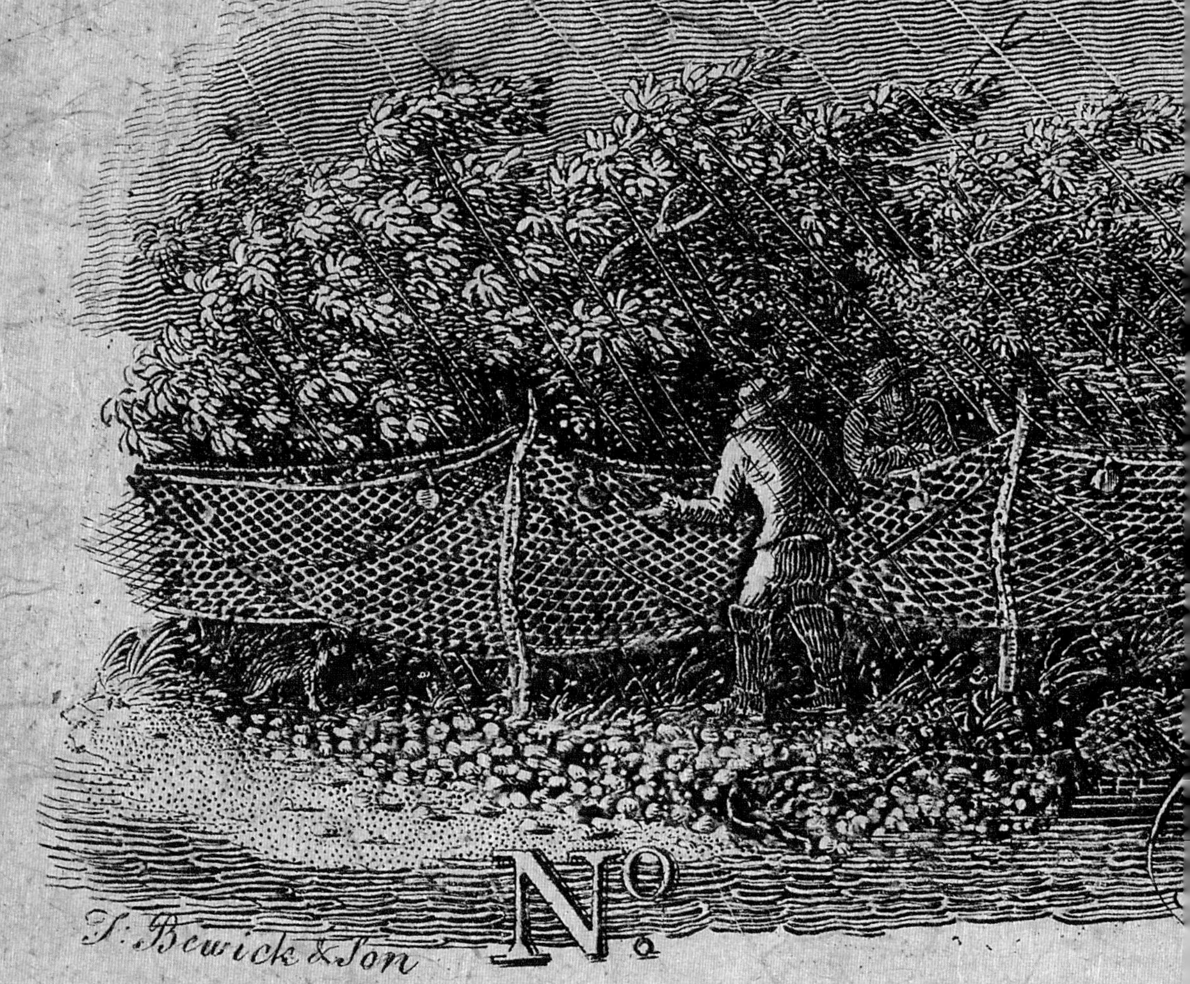
T. Bewick & Son

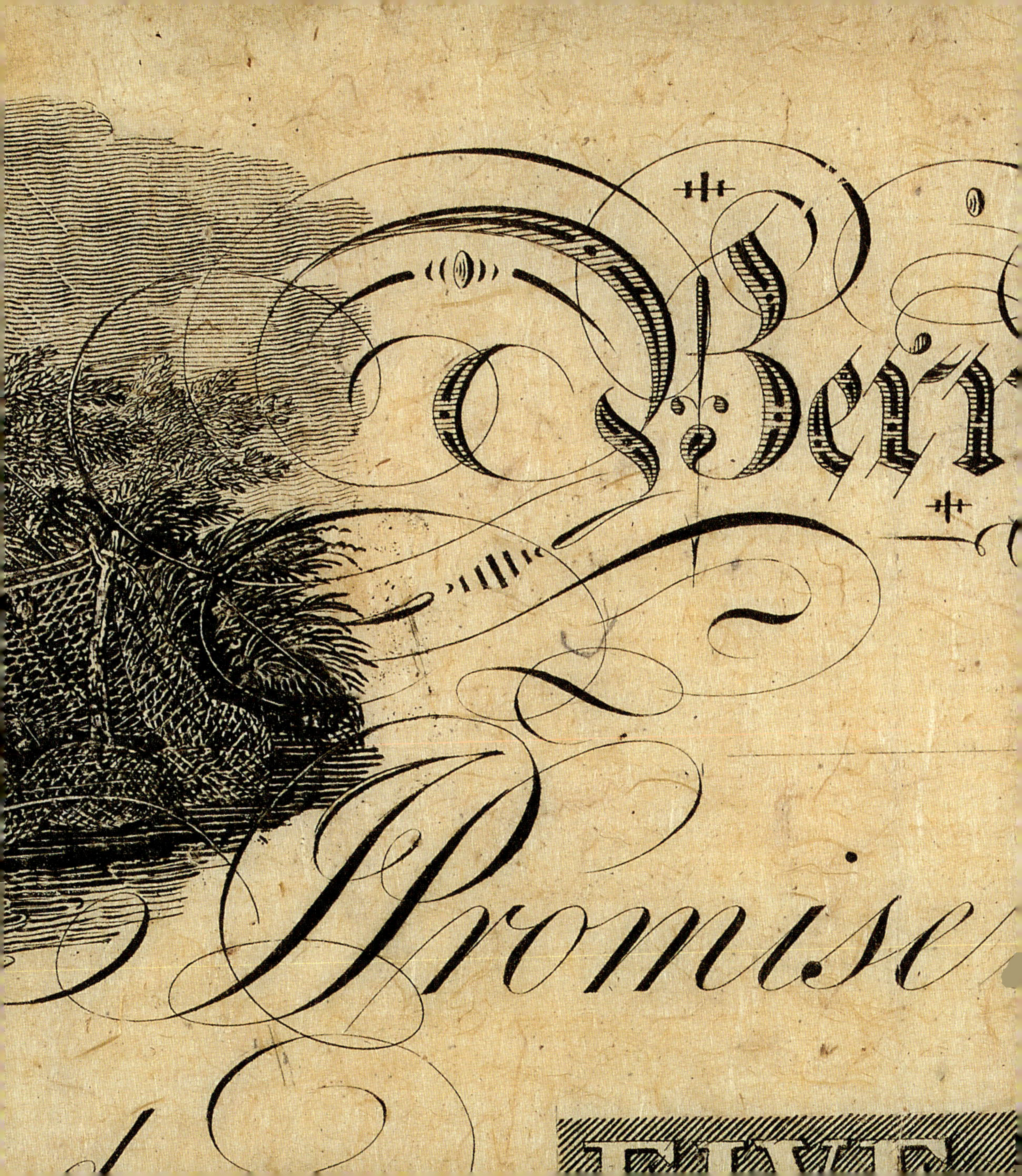
Ber
Promise

Banking

Given Ralph Beilby and Thomas Bewick's skills in engraving
on precious metals (and the trust reposed in them by the town's
goldsmiths), it was natural for the bankers of Newcastle and its
vicinity to turn to their workshop for complex (hopefully, forgery-
proof) designs on their banknotes. Unlike today, banknote design
and production were not specialized activities and it was an area
to which Bewick applied his skills relentlessly in the hope of
defeating the aspirations of counterfeiters. Other criteria had to
be borne in mind. A banknote had to express strength, wealth and
reliability; it was, after all, paper pretending to be gold. Invariably,
banknote designs were engraved upon copper with fine, elaborate
lettering and gracious motifs much in evidence and printed upon a
special paper called 'thin bank post'.

Banking had boomed in the last half of the eighteenth
century, in part because the Bank of England in London did not
have a monopoly on issuing notes. This allowed landowners and
industrialists in the provinces to create partnerships (six partners
was the legal maximum) and establish country or provincial banks
in order to generate capital for expansion. These banks played an
integral role in local economic growth and their banknotes reflect
the massive rise in industrialization across the kingdom. In 1750,
twelve such banks were in operation; by 1797 there were well over
two hundred; by 1810, in excess of seven hundred. This boom
was not an unalloyed blessing; several banks were imposters, and
Bewick suffered at the hands of one of them. Never subject to the
draconian penalties imposed upon forgers, those who established
such banks (which, when bankrupted, often took the livelihoods
and even the lives of honest merchants and traders with them)
were treated leniently by the judicial system.

Newcastle's first bank, 'The Old Bank', was founded in 1755 and
by 1789 the town supported four more. Their partners were powerful

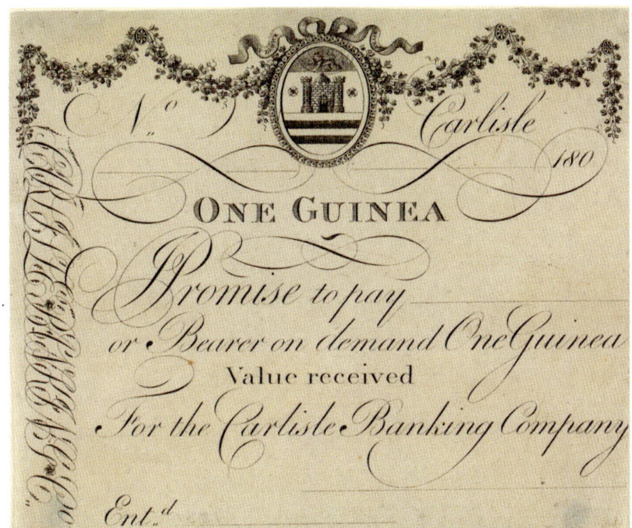

Carlisle Banking Company, one guinea banknote, designed and engraved by Bewick, 31 December 1801, at a charge of £3 3s. 0d. 120 × 140 mm. British Museum 1882,0311.3154.

colliery proprietors, bottle-glass manufacturers and landowners, local magnates who, more often than not, were connected to Newcastle's common council and ran the town as a virtual fiefdom. Their connections to the Corporation of Newcastle meant that their banks possessed a quasi-public status and the townspeople would no more question the negotiability of their banknotes than they would the paper money issued by the Bank of England (which did not open a branch in Newcastle until the late 1820s).

Forgery was endemic, despite the imposition of the death penalty. In 1801, in excess of eight thousand forged notes were detected, counterfeiting on a scale that threatened the stability of Britain's wartime economy. Penalties had little deterrent value, forgers being well aware that juries were unwilling to convict, given that the sentence of capital punishment was widely perceived as unjust. A country bank was particularly vulnerable to counterfeiting. If it refused to accept a note, word could quickly spread that the bank was unsound. The consequence would have been a run on the bank, usually with disastrous results.

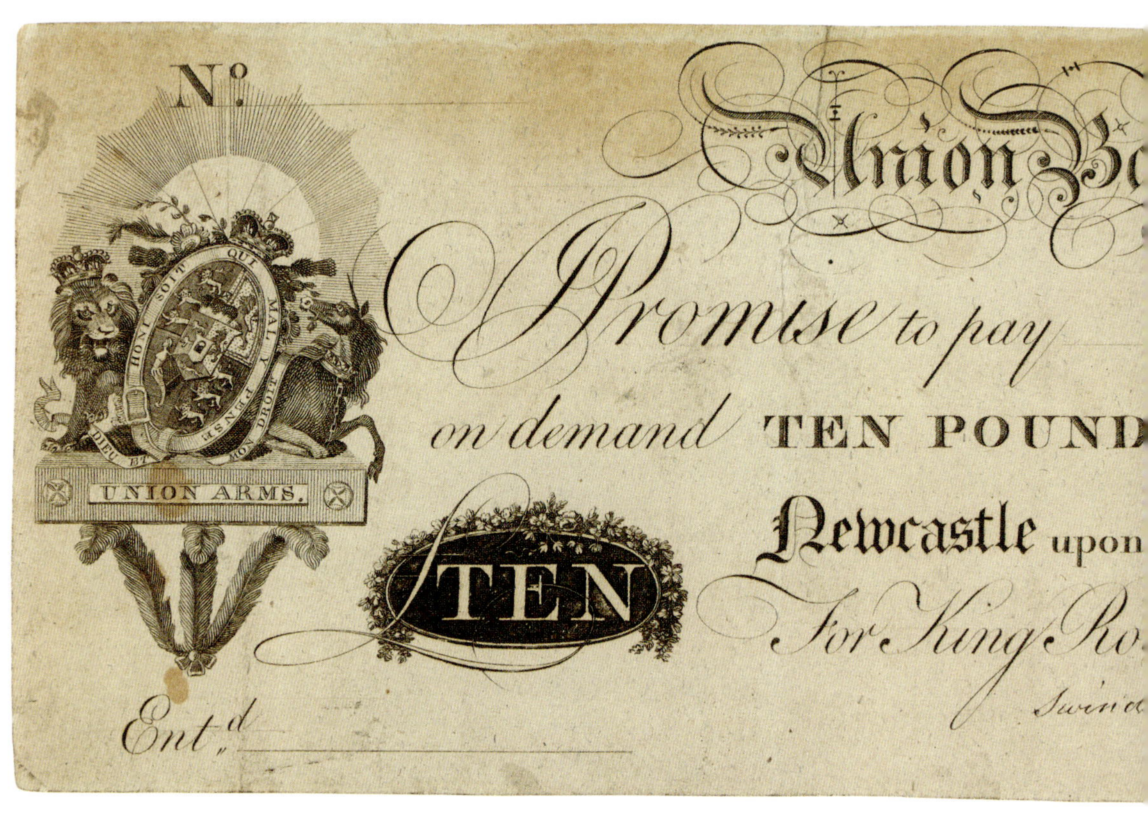

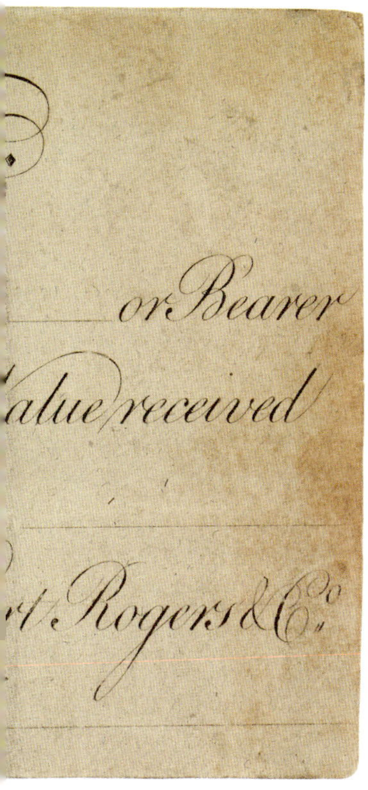

Union Bank (of London), ten pound note, designed and engraved by Bewick, 10 October 1801, at a charge of £3 3s. 0d. One of a series of three engraved and printed for Messrs King, Rochfort and Rogers of Portland Place. Alas, Jane Bewick's inscription 'Swindlers', scrawled across this example, was only too accurate. John King (born Jacob Rey), a Jewish money-lender to the indebted nobility, had recently established the bank in grand style with his so-called wife Lady Lanesborough (née Rochfort) and George Rogers (lately secretary to Admiral Lord Keppel and now a Commissioner of the Navy) as partners. Retainers were dispatched to set up branches of the bank in the foremost manufacturing districts and advertising boasted of their existence in many of 'the principal Towns', although only Derby seems to have had – albeit briefly – a branch. In 1802, shortly before its demise, the bank was described as 'a nest of miscreants' and as having a 'vast number of creditors'. Amongst them was Thomas Bewick, owed the sum of £18 for engraving and printing the notes. 96 × 200 mm. British Museum 1882,0311.3155.

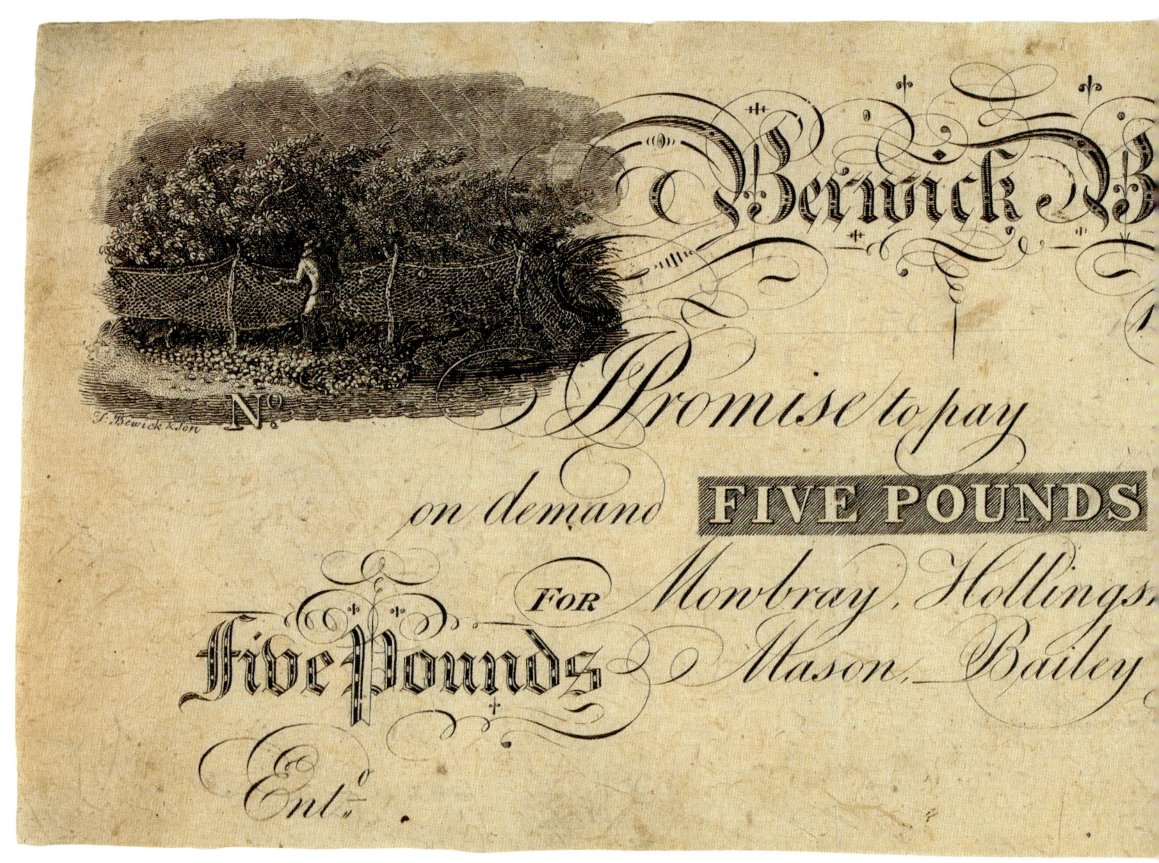
Bewick B
Promise to pay
on demand FIVE POUNDS
FOR Mowbray, Hollings
Five Pounds Mason, Bailey
Ent.
No.
T. Bewick & Son

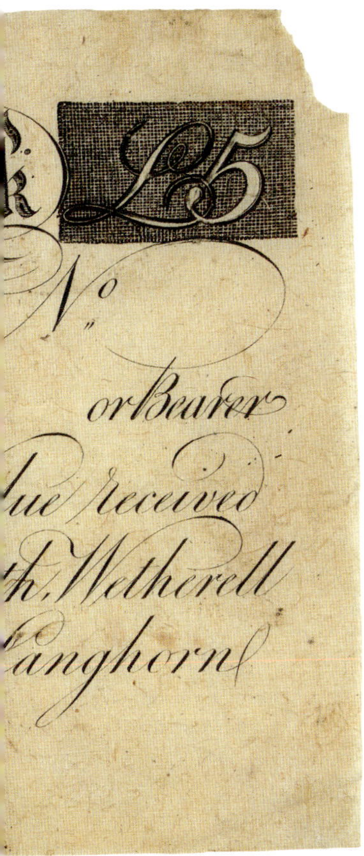

Berwick Bank, five pound note, designed and etched by Bewick, 25 September 1813, at a charge of £5 5s. 0d. Amongst the bank's partners was John Bailey, an old friend of Bewick's who had commenced life as an engraver in Durham but who made his fortune as an agriculturist and as the estate steward to Lord Tankerville at Chillingham. He complained to Bewick of the 'Pen & Ink forgeries' which had lately been committed upon the Berwick Bank and this was Bewick's response. He exercised himself greatly over the cross-hatched images, remarking the £5 device cost him 'as much labour as all the rest of the plate put together' and expressing his optimism that the note would be impossible 'for any villain to imitate'. The vignette of the fisherman drying his nets is inspired by a similar device, designed and engraved on wood in the previous week (18 September 1813), which later appeared in Bewick's *Fables of Aesop* of 1818. 110 × 205 mm. British Museum 1882,0311.3158.

Insurance

Household insurance as we know it today commenced in the immediate aftermath of the Great Fire of London when a number of marine insurance underwriters expanded their activities to satisfy domestic and business demands. By the mid-eighteenth century Newcastle, with its highly capitalized collieries and its all-too-combustible industries – chemicals, glass, pottery, lead and ironworks – had attracted the notice of the major London insurance companies and their success did not go unnoticed.

It was perhaps the profitability of the three Newcastle banking houses of the day, 'The Old Bank', the 'Exchange Bank' and the 'Tyne Bank', which persuaded several of the partners in those houses, plus representatives from the leading mercantile and industrial families on Tyneside, to invest in insurance. The result was the Newcastle upon Tyne Fire Insurance Office, a partnership with twenty proprietors and a fund of £105,000. Established in 1783, its backers included opulent colliery owner Sir Matthew White Ridley, industrialist Isaac Cookson and Rowland Burdon, projector of the famous cast-iron bridge at Sunderland. As with banking, many of the proprietors were closely associated with the Corporation of Newcastle and several represented the town and county in Parliament, thereby creating a privileged network of mutually beneficial interests. Again as with banking, the Fire Office (as it was widely termed) rapidly achieved the status of a quasi-public institution, assisted by its annexing the arms of Newcastle as its logo.

With its prominent local proprietors, vigorous advertising campaigns, widespread business connections and direct experience of the risks involved in local industries, the Fire Office rapidly supplanted almost all the other insurance firms in Newcastle and its environs. (The Beilby-Bewick workshop immediately took out insurance with it.) The concern prospered mightily, providing most

of the fire-fighting equipment in the town (the Bewick workshop
engraved its brass fire-hose couplings, clamps and nozzles with the
Fire Office name). It took over as the sole supplier of the town's
water in 1797 (it being in the Fire Office's interest to maintain a
healthy supply) and established the first gasworks in 1817 (gaslight
was safer than candlelight and allowed for another profit stream).
Two years later, Bewick installed gas to light his workshop.

As with banknotes, the designs that headed the policies
required images of strength and reassurance. In addition, the
Fire Office required woodcuts for receipts, announcements and
newspaper advertisements, for barely a week passed in which the
Fire Office failed to maintain its presence in one or another of
the local papers.

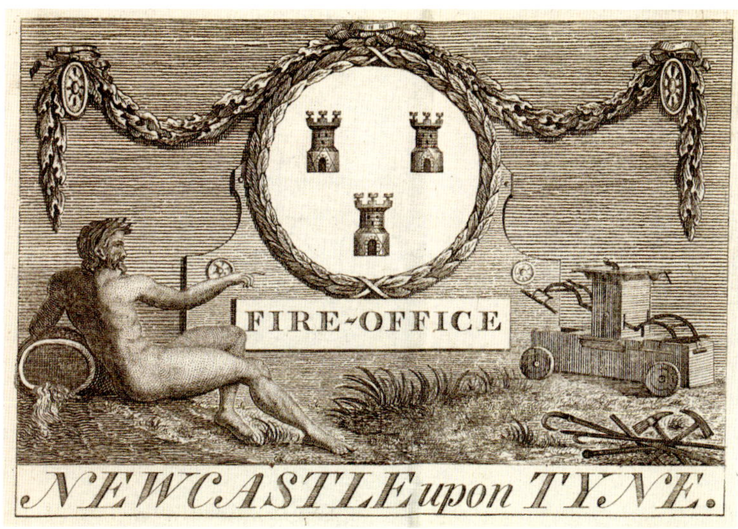

Policy heading for the Newcastle upon Tyne Fire Office, engraved on copper by Bewick, 15 February 1783, at a charge of £3 3s. 0d. The arms of Newcastle are flanked to the left by the Neptune-like figure of the river-god Tyne, to the right by a two-man pumping engine and firemen's tools. 105 × 142 mm. Private collection.

Heading for the leaf of 'Proposals' – terms and conditions –
which accompanied the policies of the Fire Office, engraved
on wood by Bewick, 4 March 1797, at a charge of £2 2s. 0d.
(and addressed to him not long thereafter). The iconography
makes explicit various commercial activities covered by the
Fire Office: shipping, cargoes and warehouse premises.
Subsequently, the woodcut headed the policies themselves
and remained in use until at least 1843. 82 × 152 mm.
British Museum 1882,03111.4567.

Policy heading for the Newcastle upon Tyne Fire Office, engraved on copper by Bewick, 29 April 1797, at a charge of £5 5s. 0d. Symbols of Newcastle, including the river-god Tyne calmly surveying the scene whilst being carried by a mythical seahorse, adorn the central pillar with valiant firefighters to the right and all hands manning the pump to the left. Serried ranks of militia have been drawn up to keep order. In the background the new building is already under construction, a comforting notion. 95 × 137 mm. Private collection.

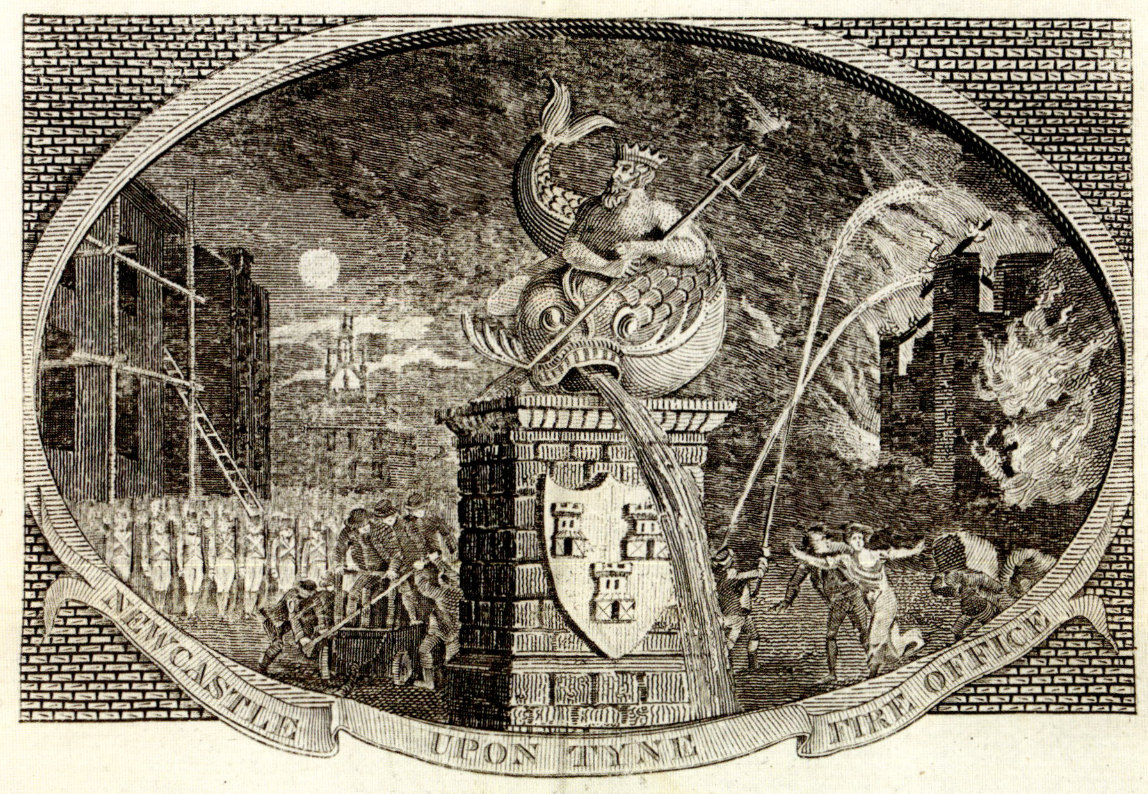

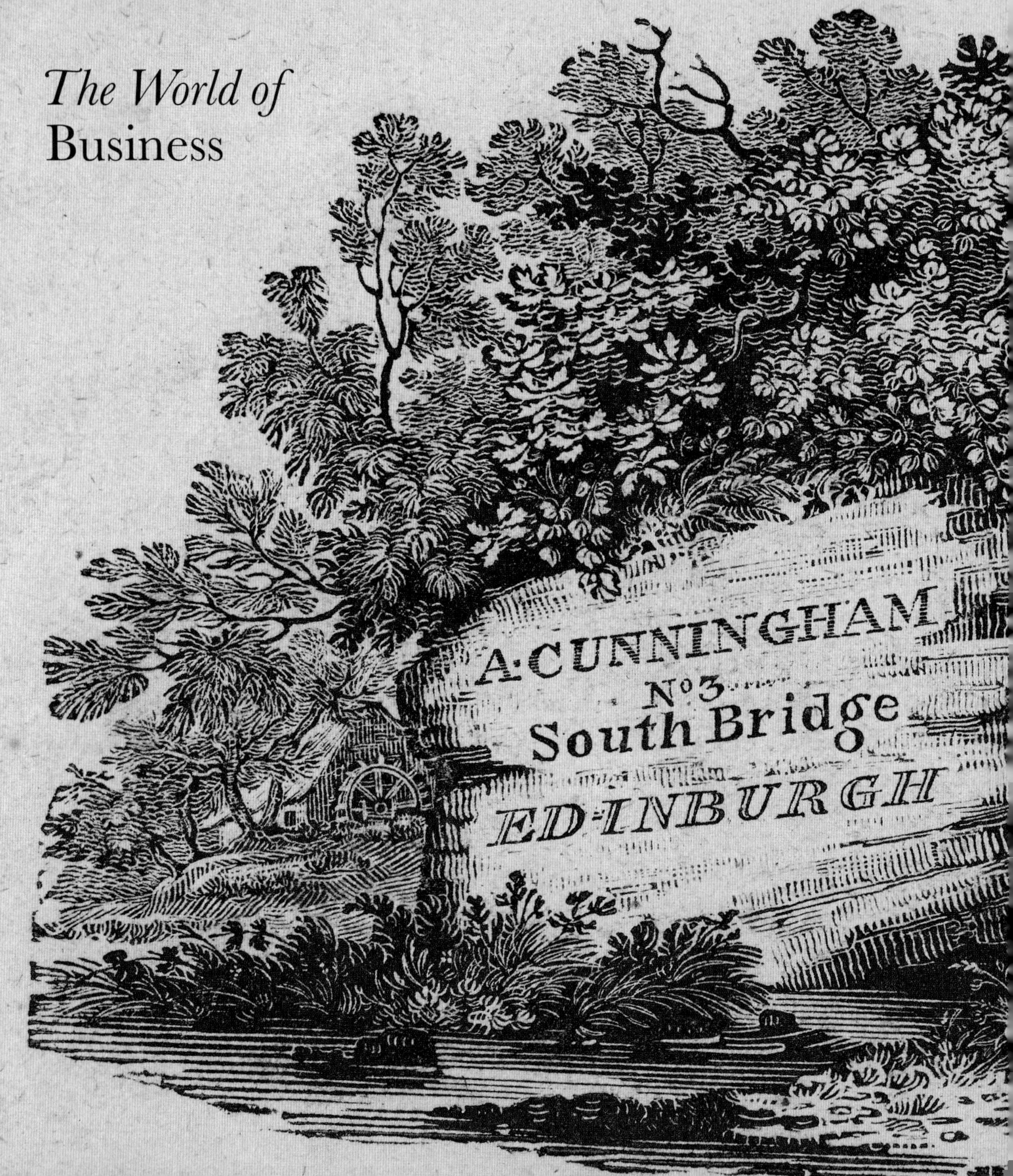
A·CUNNINGHAM
Nº3
South Bridge
EDINBURGH

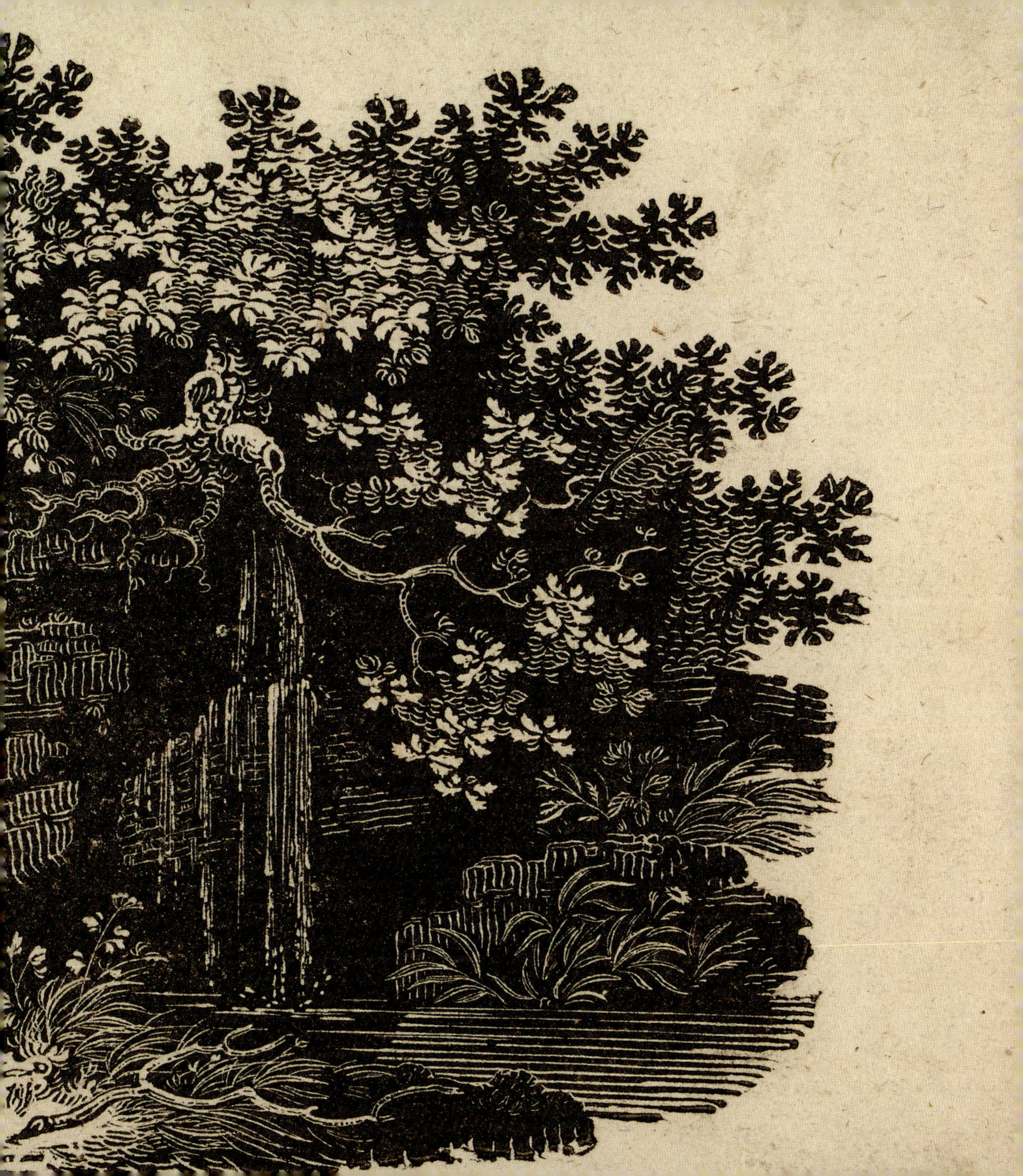

Trade Cards

Printed on paper or card as useful reminders of goods and services offered, a trade card was given out to the public rather like the ubiquitous (but less interesting) business card of today. The text frequently included, along with the name and address of the trader or retailer, an account of the various departments of the concern and a description of the quality and value for money of the goods stocked or manufactured, all composed in the most polished and deferential prose. A retailer new to the area might also add a reference to a master served in his previous employment.

Such cards often embodied an image of the signboard which hung outside the retailer's premises or which, after legislation prohibited them on safety grounds and street numbering began to be gradually introduced from the 1760s, were fixed flush to the wall – the precursor of the modern fascia. This is clearly seen in the example of the upholsterers Webster and Brown and their highly prized sign of 'The Royal Tent'. Such signs were not entirely decorative. A barely literate maidservant, despatched by her mistress to pick up a sample of cloth from the upholsterers, would have found it easier to locate a sign than a number or name.

From the 1780s, the fashion of framing the details within elements of polite ornament and design, such as rococo mirror frames or neoclassical columns, started to wane and a specific imagery – reflecting the belief that a picture is worth a thousand words – gradually emerged. This continued to emphasize the quality of the goods and services on offer, but played upon the subtler principle that less is more.

Card for Webster and Brown engraved on copper by Ralph Beilby in his most elaborate style, 30 July 1770, at a charge of £2 12s. 6d. The images of crescent moon, stars and sun appear to have been added in pencil by Ralph Beilby himself. 186 × 136 mm. British Museum Banks, 28.149.

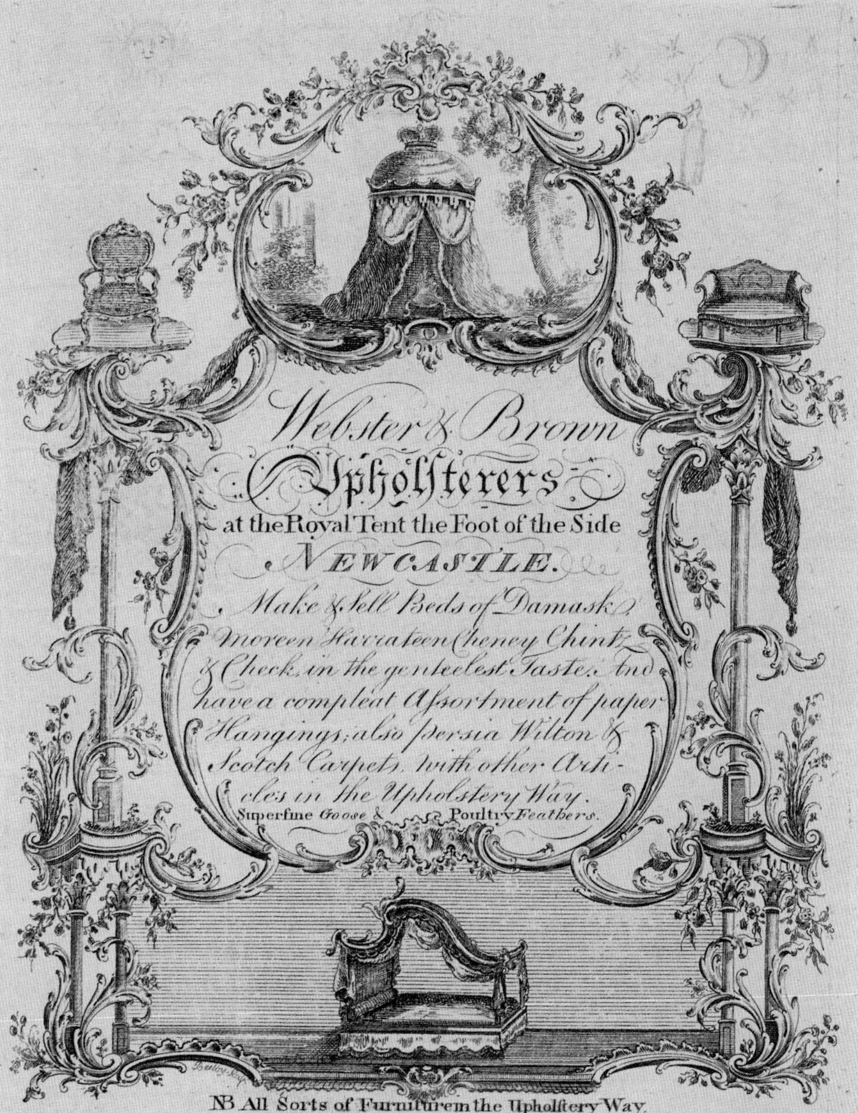

Webster & Brown
Upholsterers
at the Royal Tent the Foot of the Side
NEWCASTLE.
Make & sell Beds of Damask
Moreen Harrateen Cheney Chintz
& Check, in the genteelest Taste. And
have a compleat Assortment of paper
Hangings: also Persia Wilton &
Scotch Carpets, with other Arti-
cles in the Upholstery Way.
Superfine Goose & Poultry Feathers.
NB All Sorts of Furniture in the Upholstery Way.
exactly match'd & neatly put up.

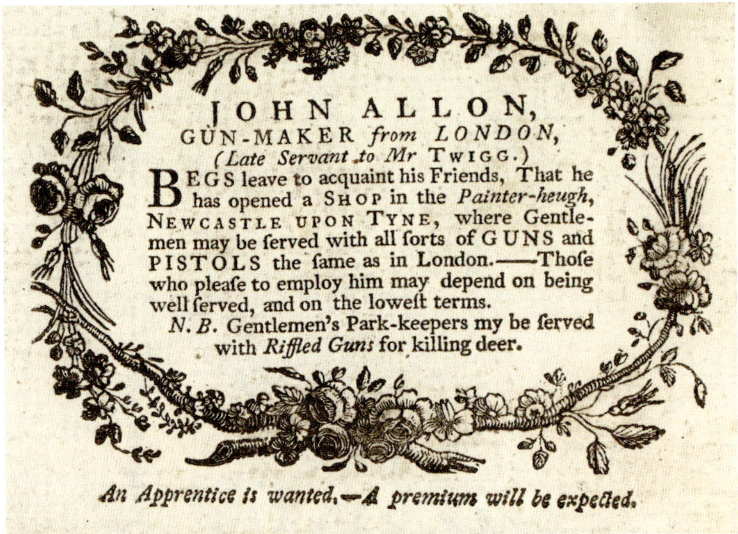

The border to John Allon's card was an all-purpose device engraved by Bewick for printer Thomas Robson, 30 September 1777, at a charge of 10s. 6d. It was an interim measure, Allon having recently arrived from London where he had worked for John Twigg, one of the most important English gunsmiths of the day. 80 × 120 mm. Private collection.

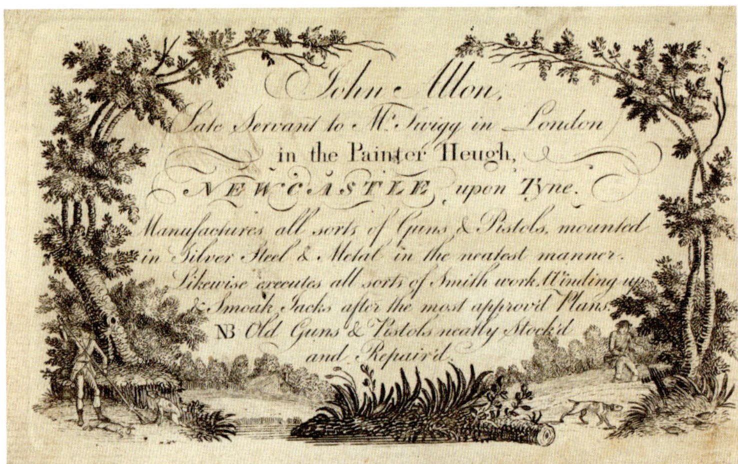

John Allon's trade card proper, engraved on copper by Bewick, 25 June 1778, at a charge of 15s. Allon's business flourished and he commissioned much 'gun-work' from the Bewick workshop, mostly engraved barrels, locks and stocks. In 1780 he advertised 'rifled pieces for … shooting seals'. He prospered until about 1802 but in January 1807 Bewick noted he 'died very poor', owing him six shillings. 75 × 123 mm. Private collection.

Card for William How,
etched(?) on copper
by Beilby, 14 June 1779,
at a charge of 15s. The
same William How, when
proprietor of the George
Inn at Penrith in 1767,
had commissioned a
bill of fare heading from
the newly apprenticed
Bewick (see p. 84).
William How took over
the Bush Inn at Carlisle
from his father-in-law in
December 1776.
75 × 117 mm. British
Museum 1882,0311.3151.

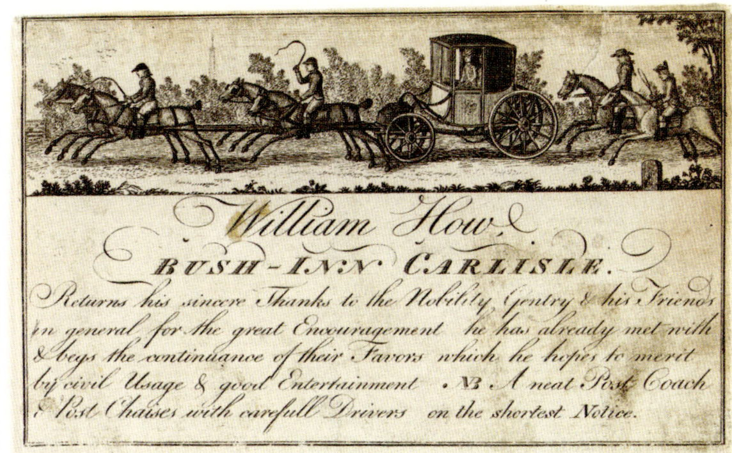

Pictorial card for William
Joyce, engraved on
copper by Bewick, 8 July
1780, at a charge of 12s.
Joyce established himself
in around 1750 and is
believed to have been an
early mentor of Lancelot
'Capability' Brown,
another Northumbrian.
65 × 95 mm. Private
collection.

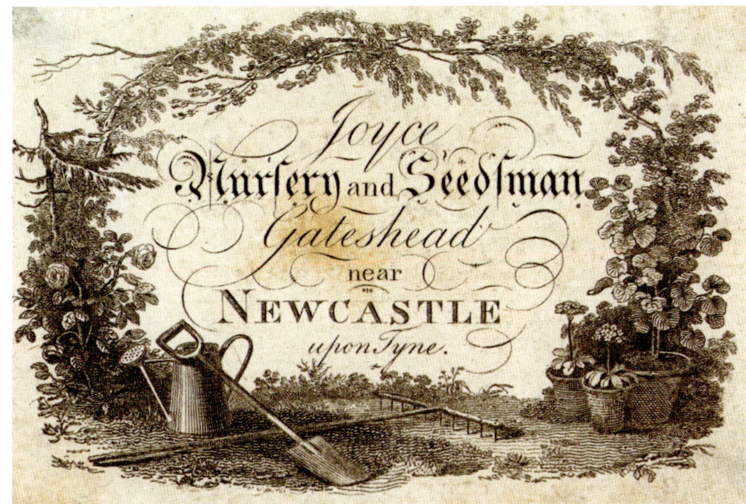

Greenwell and Brown's card, engraved on copper around May 1781 by Bewick, shortly after the business was established. Their trade card, sparse in its detail, was continuously supplemented by advertising in the local papers. For example, in June 1781 they advertised they had just taken deliveries 'from the different Manufactories of London, Birmingham and Sheffield of an elegant assortment of Japann'd Tea Urns, Coffee pots, Tea Trays and Waiters, of entire new and fashionable patterns: a great variety of Prince's Metal Candlesticks, Shovels and Tongs, Fenders with Locks and every kind of Iron and Brass Work necessary for Buildings. A genteel assortment of Ladies and Gentlemen's Riding Whips, with every Article of the Sadlery Branch, in the new and most fashionable taste.' 88 × 58 mm. British Museum, London 1882,0311.3149

Francis Howson's card, engraved on copper by Bewick, c. 1796. Richard Raithby was an eminent saddler in London's prestigious Piccadilly and receives almost equal prominence. 80 × 62 mm. British Museum 1882,0311.3150.

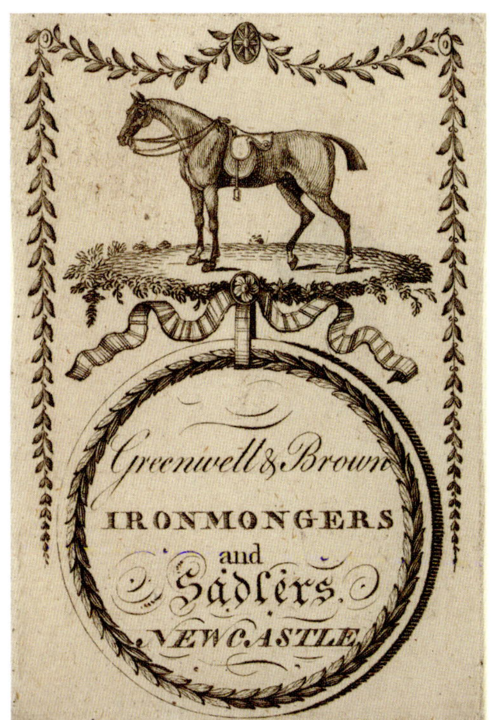

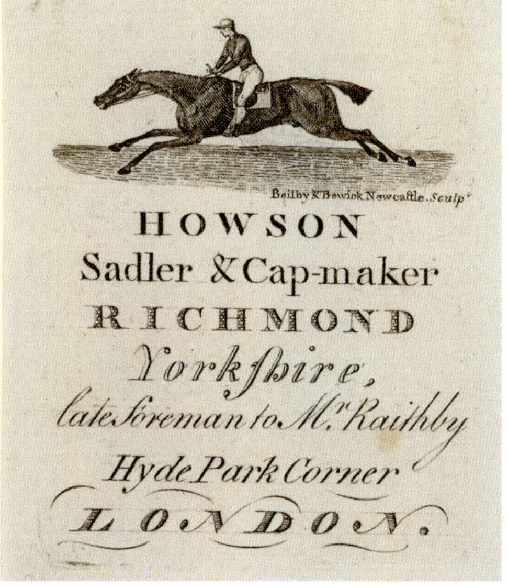

Matthew Gregson's card, engraved on wood by Bewick, 19 October 1793, at a charge of £1 11s. 6d. 90 × 130 mm. British Museum 1882,0311.2413.

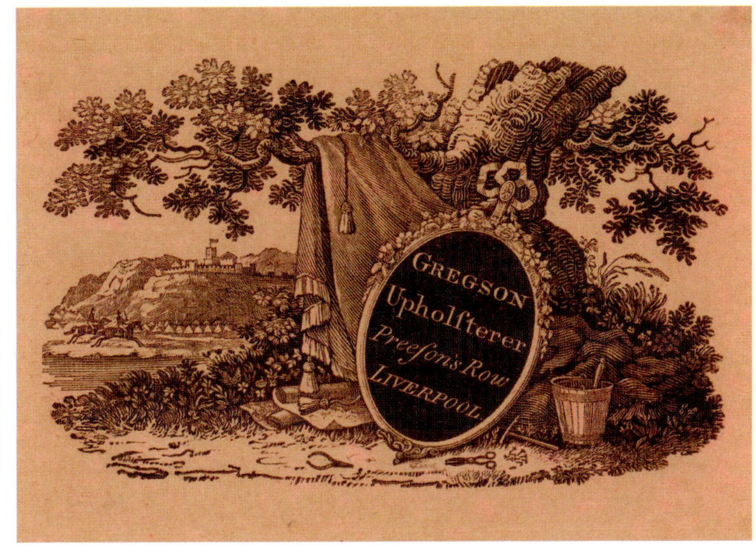

Alexander Cunningham's card, engraved on wood by Bewick, 13 July 1799, at an approximate charge of £2 2s. 0d. One of Edinburgh's foremost jewellers and medallists, Cunningham's pre-eminence excused him any need to state his business. An average of 350 cards were ordered every year. 95 × 140 mm. British Museum 1882,0311.3222.

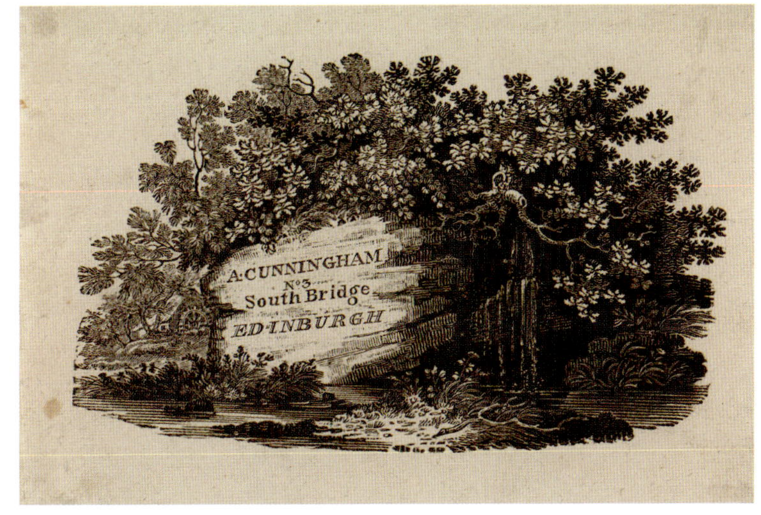

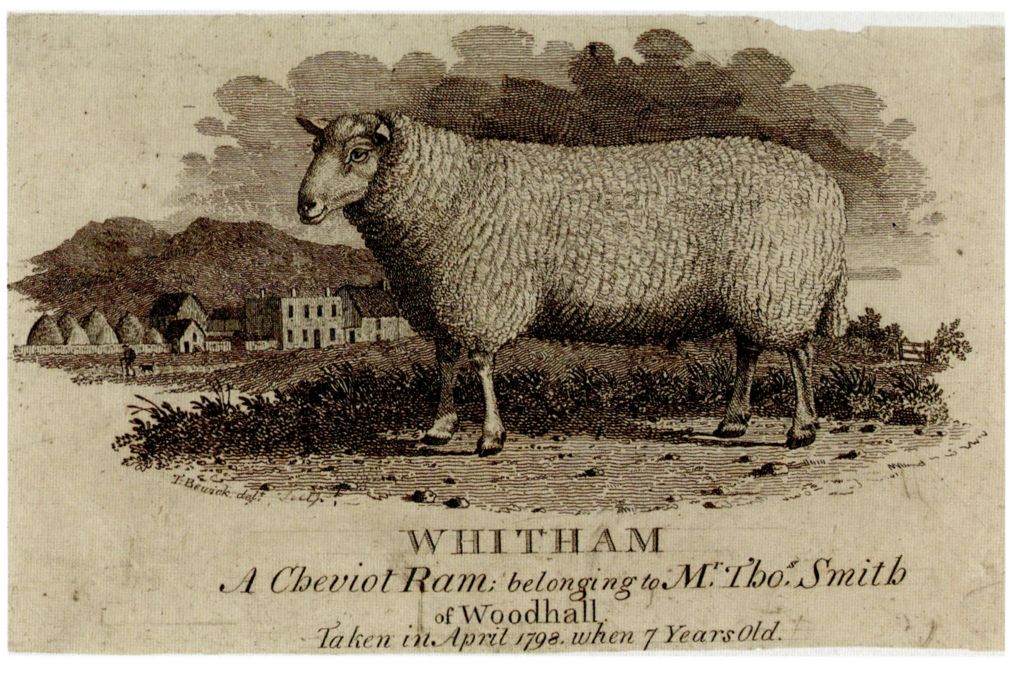

Stud card for stockbreeder Thomas Smith of Woodhall,
etched and engraved on copper by Bewick, 5 May 1798.
Although Newcastle was best known as an industrial
centre, Northumberland was home to many agricultural
improvers and stockbreeders. 95 × 140 mm.
British Museum 1882,0311.4455.

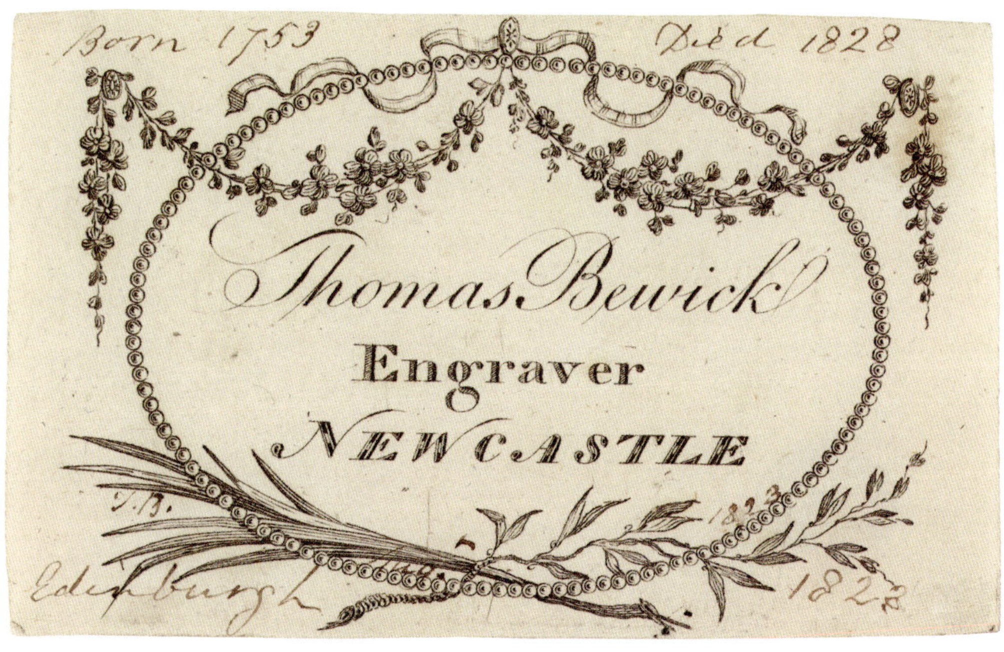

Bewick's own card, engraved on copper for his visit to
Edinburgh in 1823 and inscribed after his death by his
daughter Jane Bewick. 56 × 90 mm.
British Museum 1882,0311.3145.

Billheads

As shopping developed and retailers became more sophisticated, so paperwork followed suit. By the 1770s no self-respecting merchant, trader or retailer could scribble out a hasty invoice on a scrap of handy paper and expect to be taken seriously. Like the trade card (the design of which it often followed in style and iconography), an engraved heading for invoices (a billhead) was intended, by the use of fine copperplate script and elegant flourishes, to complement the civility of the shopkeeper and reflect the discrimination of the customer. As Bewick's skill as an illustrator spread, enterprising retailers and traders increasingly commissioned illustrations of their premises or services to feature on their billheads.

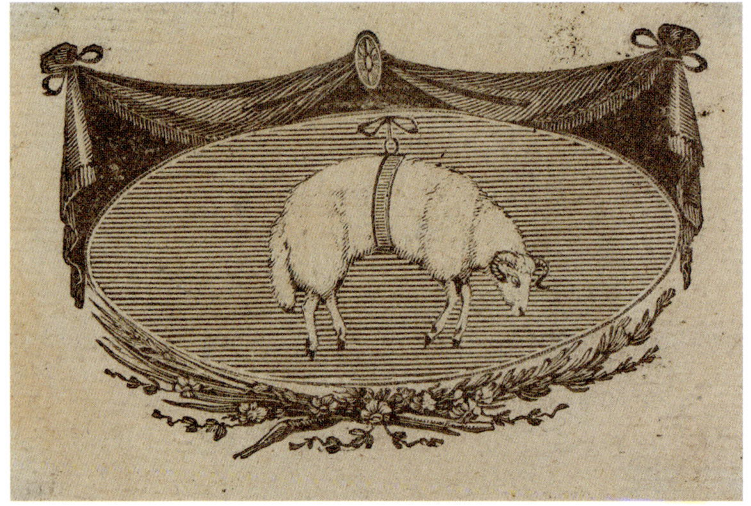

Wood engraving by Bewick for an unidentified woollen draper, *c.* 1789. The image probably reflected a hanging sign, perhaps 'The Golden Fleece'. The text of the invoice (name and address) would have been printed letterpress in the usual manner. 60 × 84 mm. British Museum 1882,0311.4885.

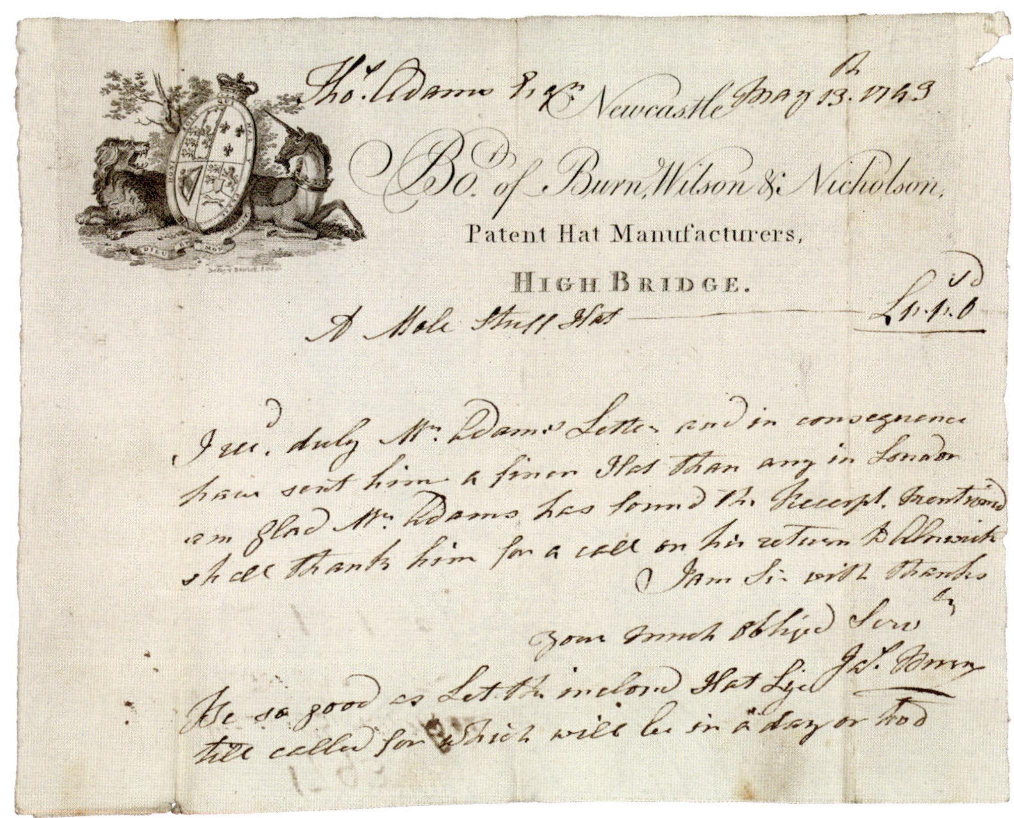

Billhead for Burn, Wilson and Nicholson, engraved on copper in the workshop, 12 May 1792, at a charge of 15s. The 'Nicholson' element was a later addition, engraved 19 January 1793, at a charge of 5s. Their shop sign was the royal coat of arms, frequently annexed without justification, but not the case here. On their establishing premises in Newcastle in May 1792, the retailers advertised their 'Manufactory of Hats, of an entire new construction, of which the delicate Fur of the Mole is the stamina, for which invention they have had the honour to retain His Majesty's Royal Letters Patent.' Thomas Adams, to whom this invoice is addressed, was a wealthy Newcastle lawyer. 100 × 205 mm. Private collection.

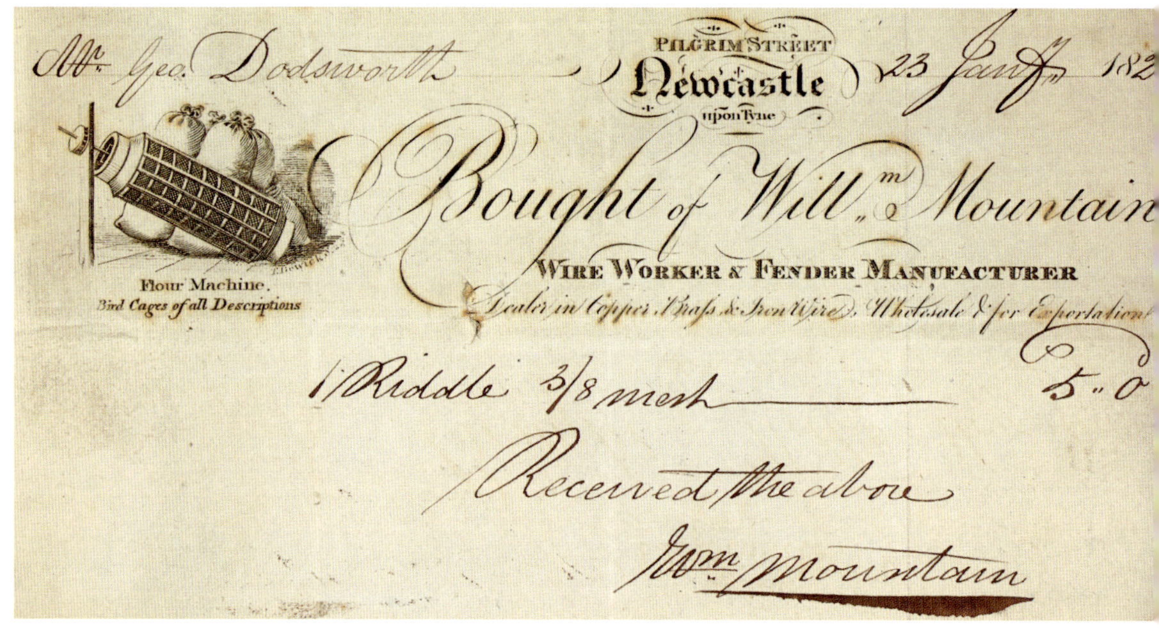

William Mountain's billhead, engraved on copper by
Bewick, 6 December 1800, at a charge of 18s. 6d.
George Dodsworth, to whom this invoice is addressed,
was proprietor of the Queen's Head in Pilgrim Street, a
thriving coaching inn. 70 × 200 mm. Private collection.

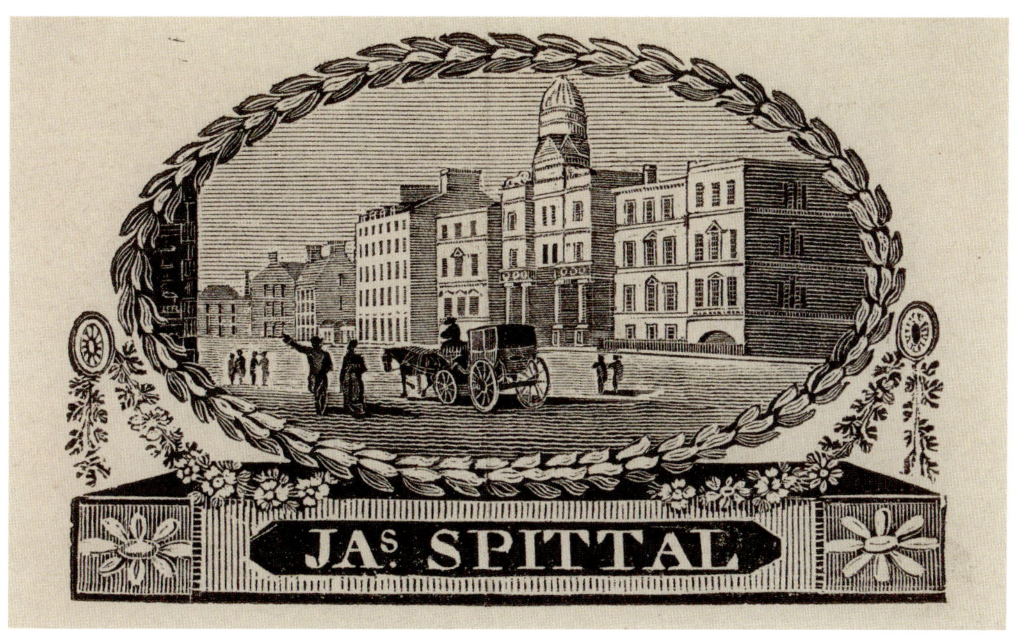

Device for James Spittal, silk merchant of 84, South
Bridge, Edinburgh, engraved on wood by Bewick,
3 November 1802, at a charge of £1 11s. 6d. Spittal's
'Fashionable Gallery' at the sign of the Golden Balloon
was a place of resort for wealthy ladies with its tempting
'Real Indian' shawls, pelisse cloths and silk hosiery. It
stood opposite Robert Adam's domed University of
Edinburgh, the building shown here (although the dome,
curiously, was not added until 1887). 65 × 90 mm.
British Museum 1882,0311.2417.

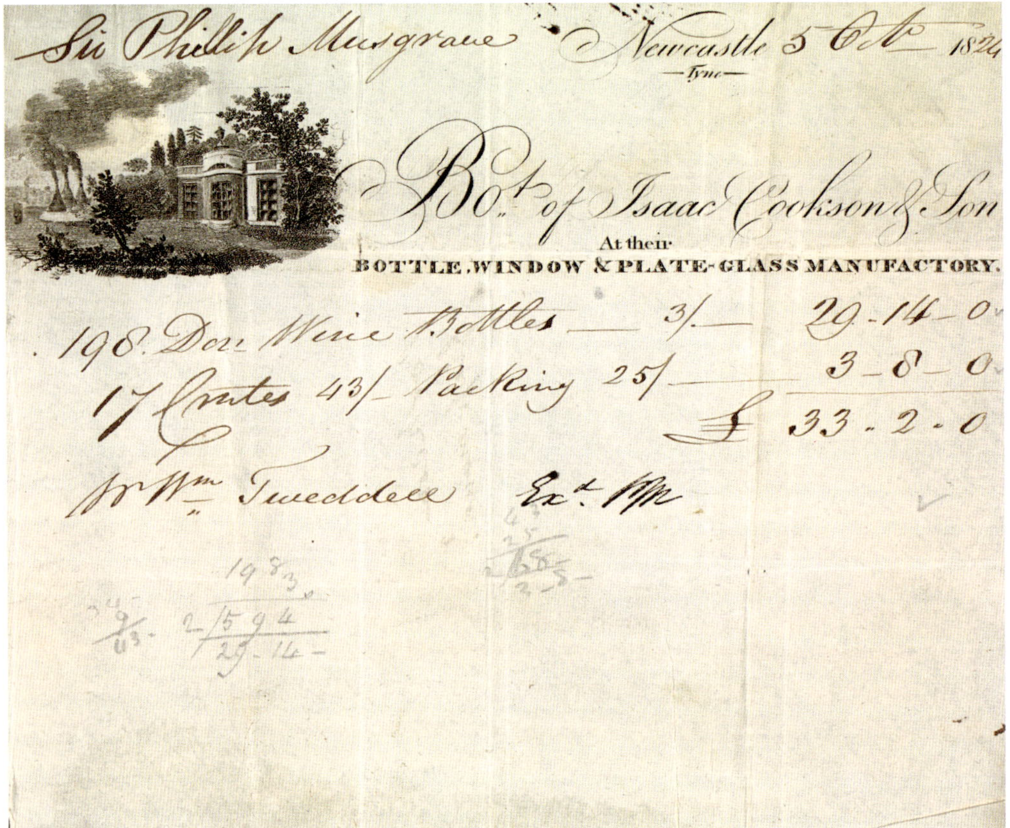

Billhead for Isaac Cookson and Son, the lettering engraved on copper in the Bewick workshop, 20 June 1807, at a charge of 10s., the device also on copper, 24 September 1814, at a charge of £1 1s. 0d. A prominent family of Newcastle bankers and industrialists, the Cooksons were proud of their achievements, despite the resulting pollution that blighted Tyneside. 109 × 205 mm. Private collection.

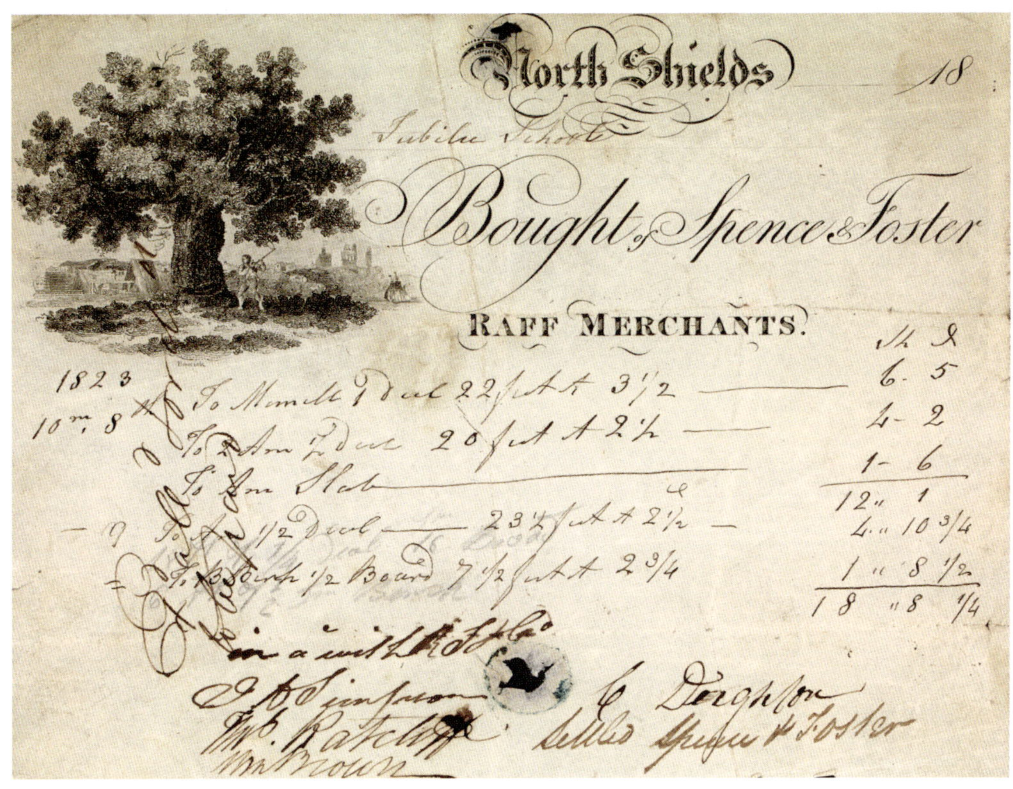

Billhead for timber merchants Robert Spence and Myles Birket Foster, engraved on copper by Robert Bewick, 3 April 1819, at a charge of £3 3s. 0d. Their premises, glimpsed in the background, included a yard for water-seasoning timber in the Tyne. Foster was the father of the renowned Victorian watercolourist of the same name. 160 × 202 mm. Private collection.

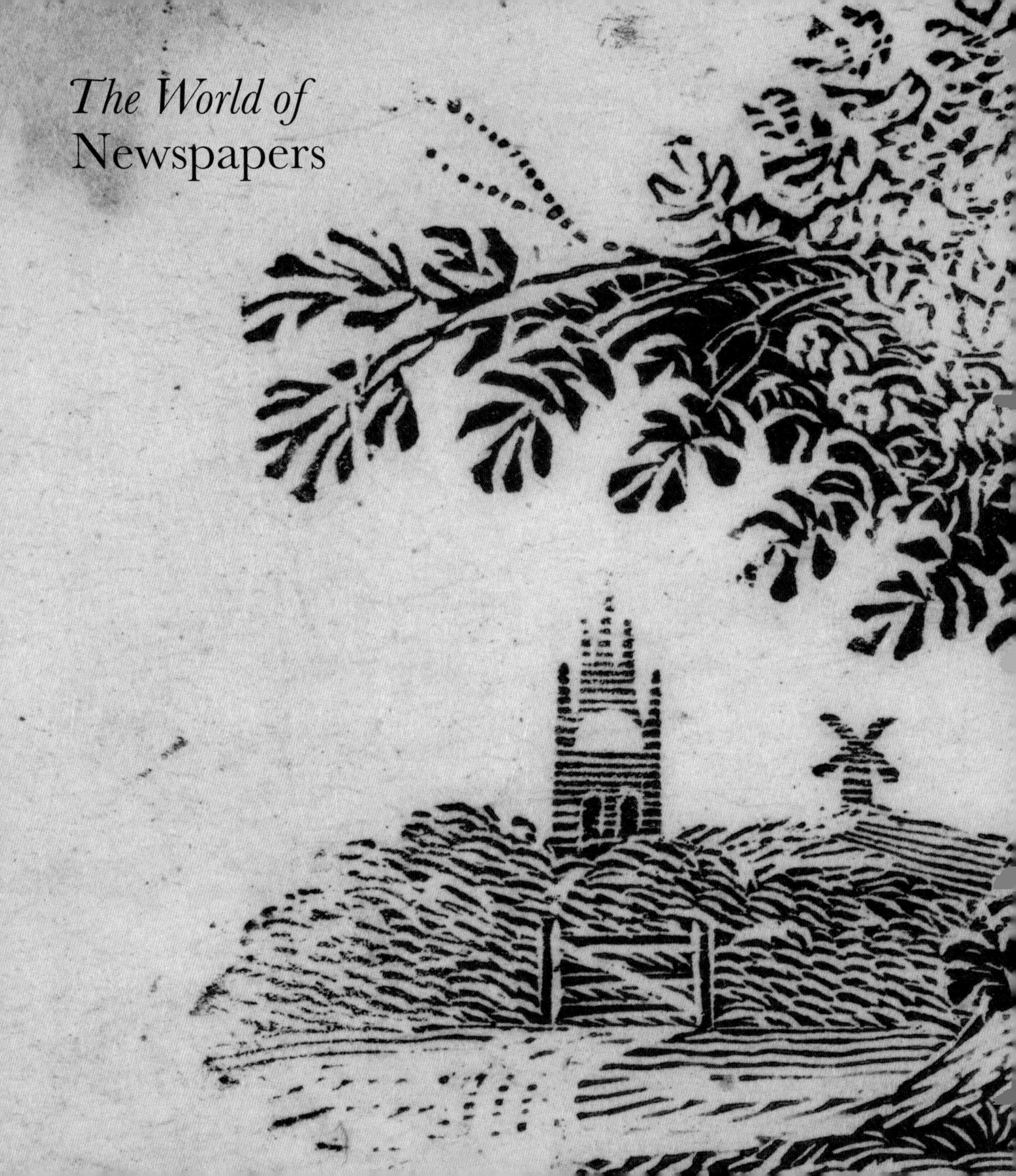
The World of
Newspapers

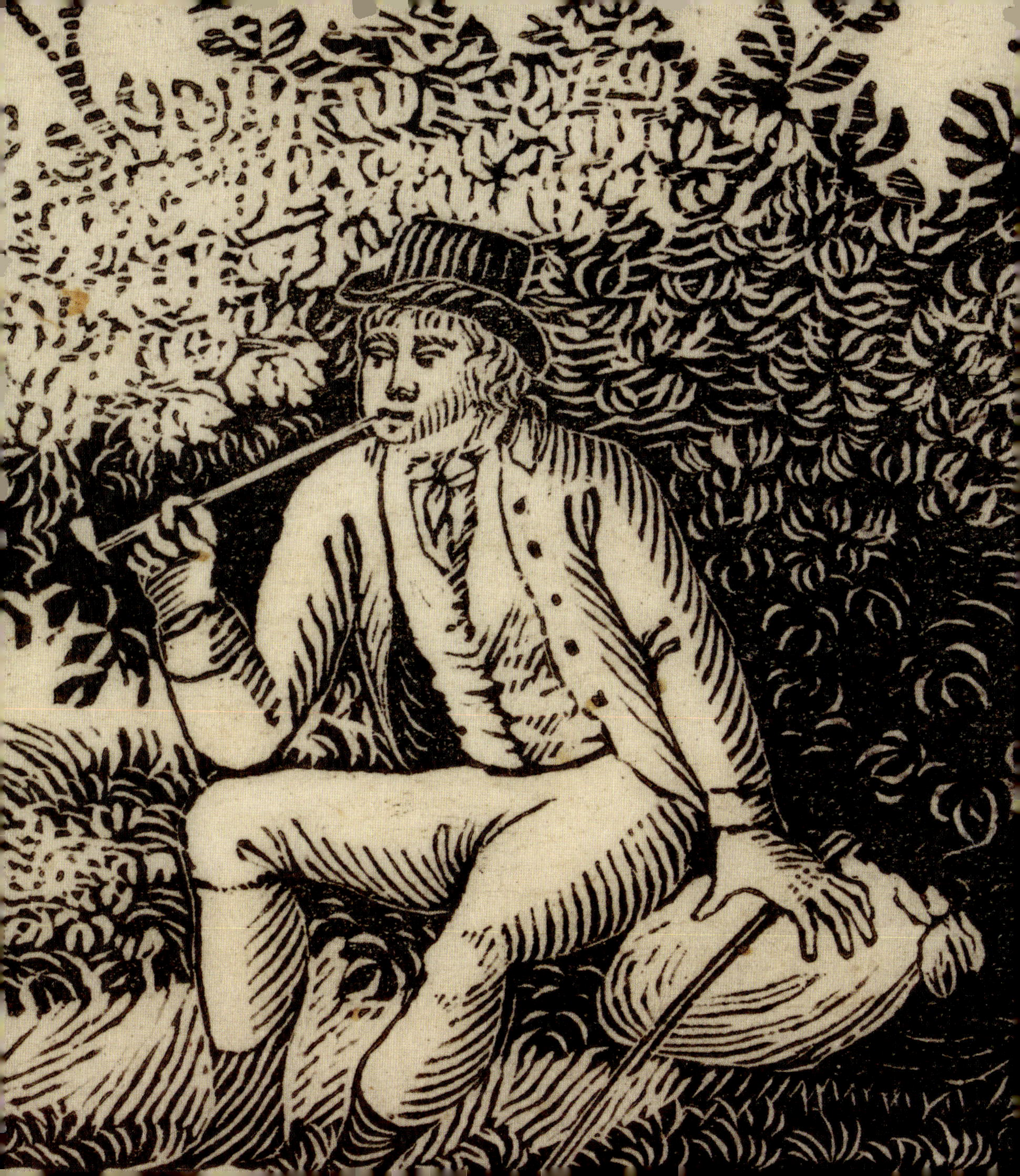

Mastheads

As newspapers proliferated in the second half of the eighteenth century, proprietors sought to distinguish their publications from the rest and the result was the development of the eye-catching masthead or banner. Whether typographic or illustrative (or both), it was intended to encapsulate the spirit of a newspaper's character and, if a country or provincial newspaper, to reflect its origin and local readership. Until the early 1800s, country newspapers were weeklies, usually appearing every Saturday. They were a far cry from a twenty-first-century daily with its plethora of supplements, being generally broadsheet in format and just four pages in length. The front page was entirely given over to advertising and official announcements, the inner pages to news domestic and foreign, shipping news, births, deaths and marriages, and correspondence; more advertising dominated the back page. Advertising, it can be seen, was the basis of the newspaper of the day. The bulk of it was plain, unvarnished text but small woodcut illustrations started to appear by the middle of the eighteenth century, perhaps a ship to illustrate shipping news, a cut of Britannia for domestic news, a waggon for a carrier's announcement, or a horse for racing results.

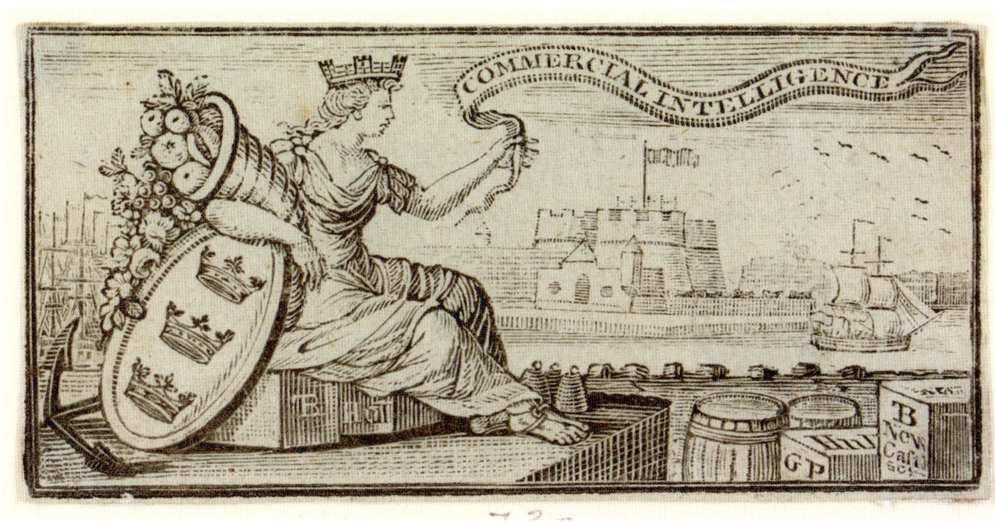

Device for the *Hull Packet*, engraved on wood by
Bewick, 19 December 1787, at a charge of 18s. Amongst
the chests awaiting shipment can be glimpsed
Thomas Bewick's initials, plus those of George Prince,
proprietor of the *Packet*. 43 × 85 mm. British Museum
1882,0311.3216.

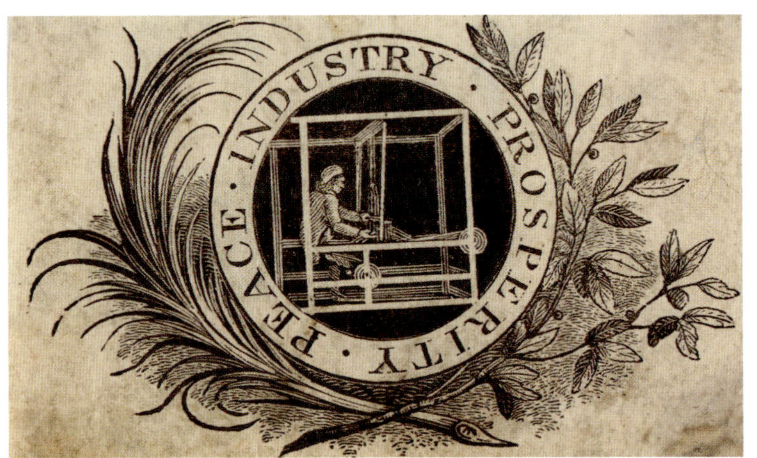

Device for the
Manchester Gazette,
engraved on wood by
Bewick, 17 October 1795,
at a charge of 15s.
46 × 75 mm. British
Museum 1882,0311.4553.

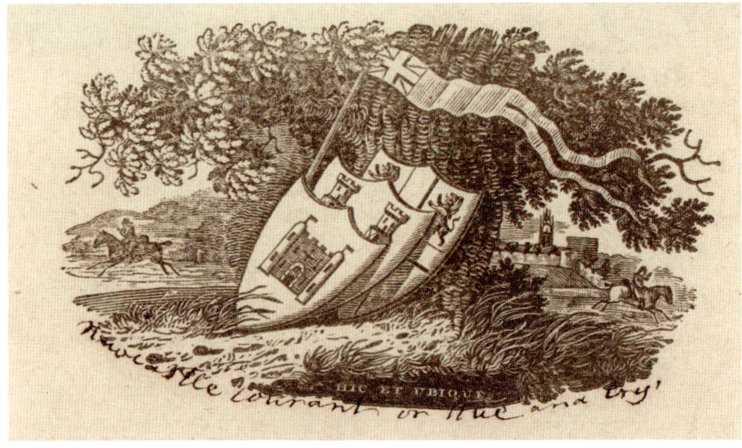

Device for the
Newcastle Courant,
engraved on wood by
Bewick, 20 February 1796,
at a charge of 12s.
50 × 75 mm. British
Museum 1882,0311.3210.

Device for the *Carlisle Journal and Northern Literary Intelligencer*, engraved on wood by Bewick, 13 July 1798, at a charge of £1 11s. 6d. The note 'Carlisle Journal' is in Bewick's hand. 50 × 95 mm. British Museum 1882,0311.3212.

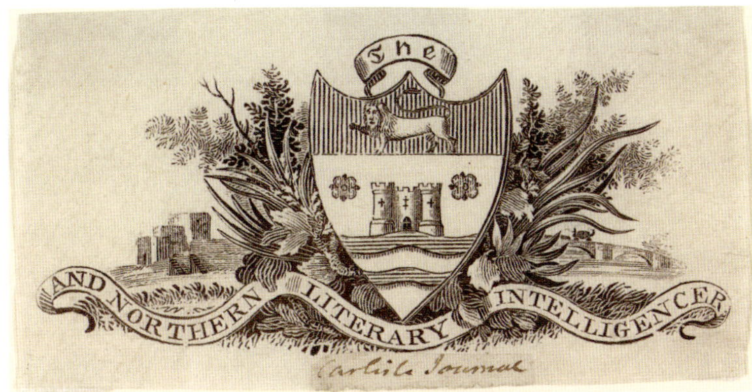

Device for *The Alfred; West of England Journal*, engraved on wood in the Bewick workshop, 2 August 1817, at a charge of £2. 70 × 95 mm. British Museum 1882,0311.4549.

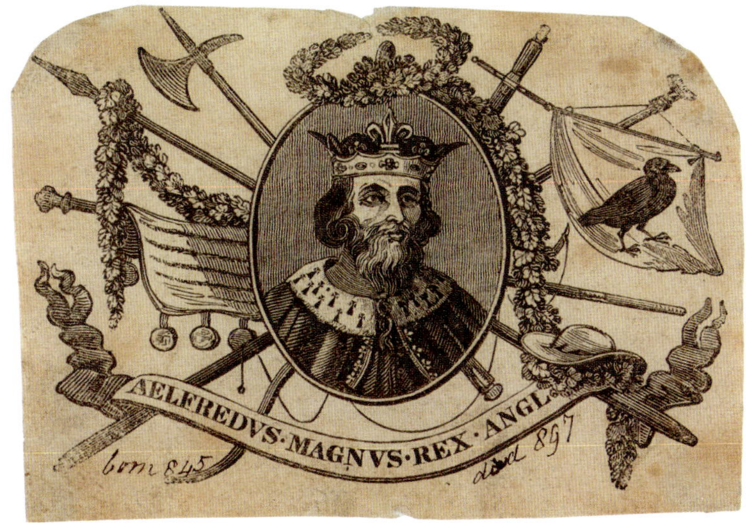

Column headings

Editorial headings were generally typeset, but added graphic devices gradually gained favour towards the end of the eighteenth century.

Device for 'Yorick's Budget', a column of miscellanea in the *Tyne Mercury*, engraved on wood by Bewick in September 1805.
45 × 72 mm. British Museum 1882,0311.4563.

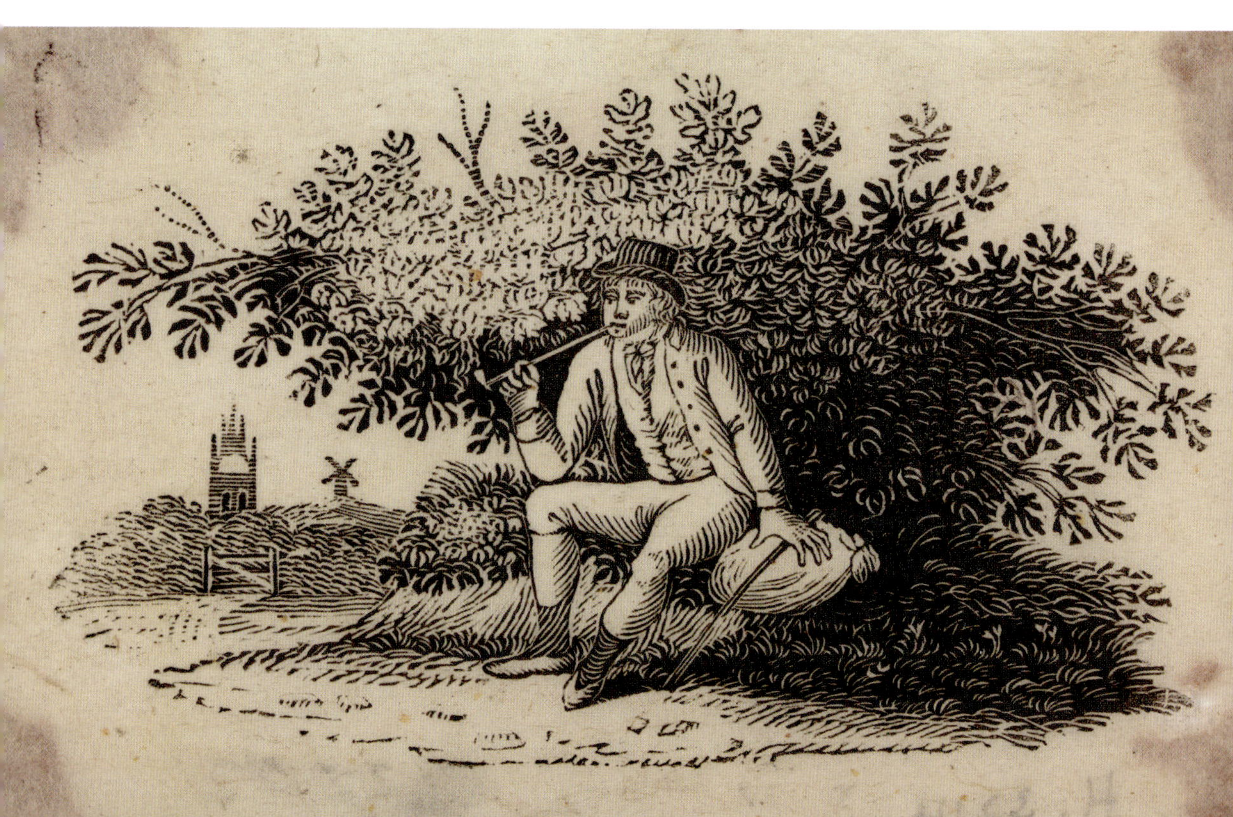

Advertisements

Newspapers provided an ideal marketplace for all goods and services and their illustrative content was largely found within the ranks of small ads.

Cockfighting had a huge following and Bewick himself 'dearly loved a main of cocks'. Illustration for a small ad, engraved on wood by Bewick, *c.* 1775, and signed in the block. Newcastle boasted at least eight cockfighting pits at the time. 38 × 58 mm. British Museum 1882,0311.3221.

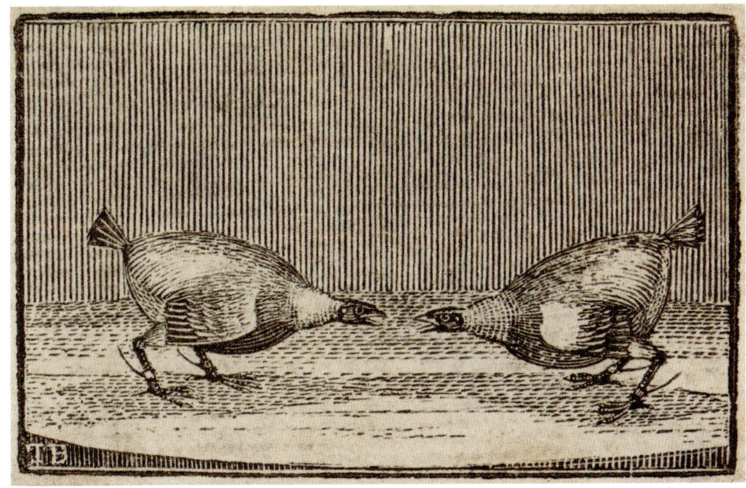

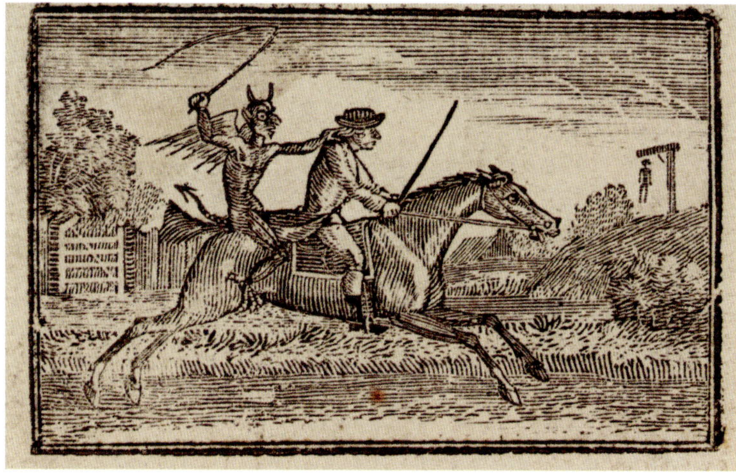

'Lost, stolen or strayed' heading, engraved on wood by Bewick, probably for Nathaniel Thorne of Durham, 25 September 1779, at a charge of 5s. The background gibbet (much favoured by Bewick as a visual motif) shows the fate of the horse thief. 40 × 70 mm. British Museum 1882,0311.3761.

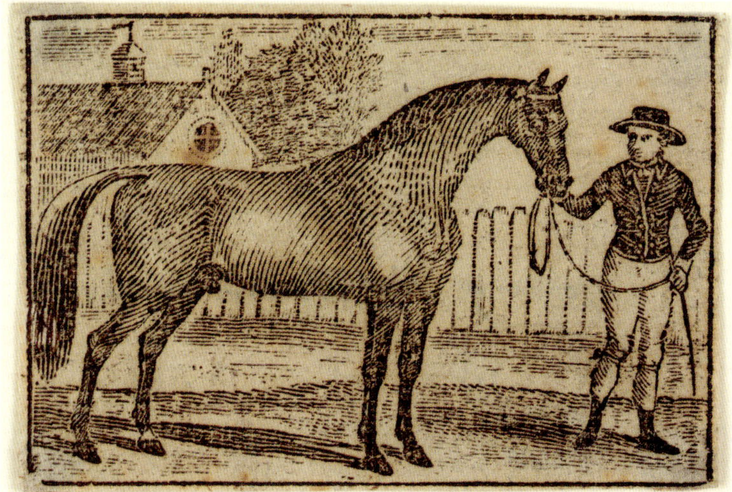

'Young Northumberland', a renowned racehorse, engraved on wood by Bewick, March 1789, to accompany a notice that the horse was now at stud. 43 × 61 mm. British Museum 1882,0311.3223.

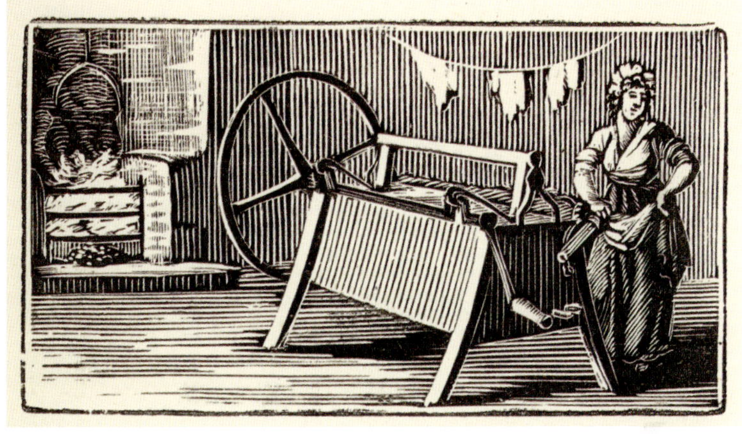

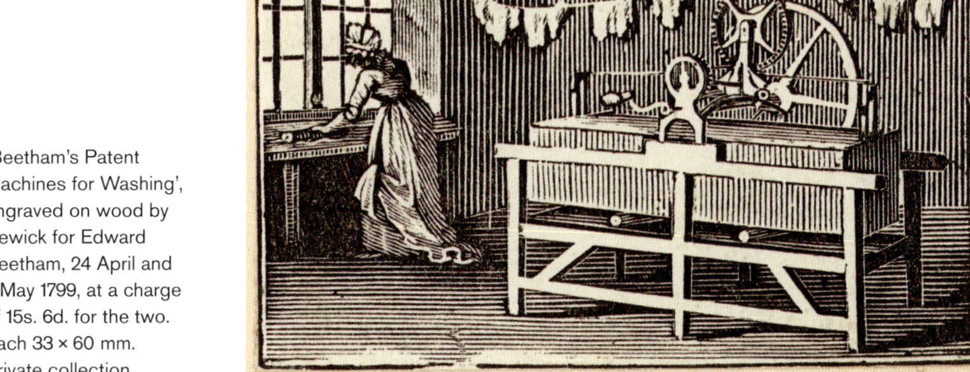

'Beetham's Patent Machines for Washing', engraved on wood by Bewick for Edward Beetham, 24 April and 6 May 1799, at a charge of 15s. 6d. for the two. Each 33 × 60 mm. Private collection.

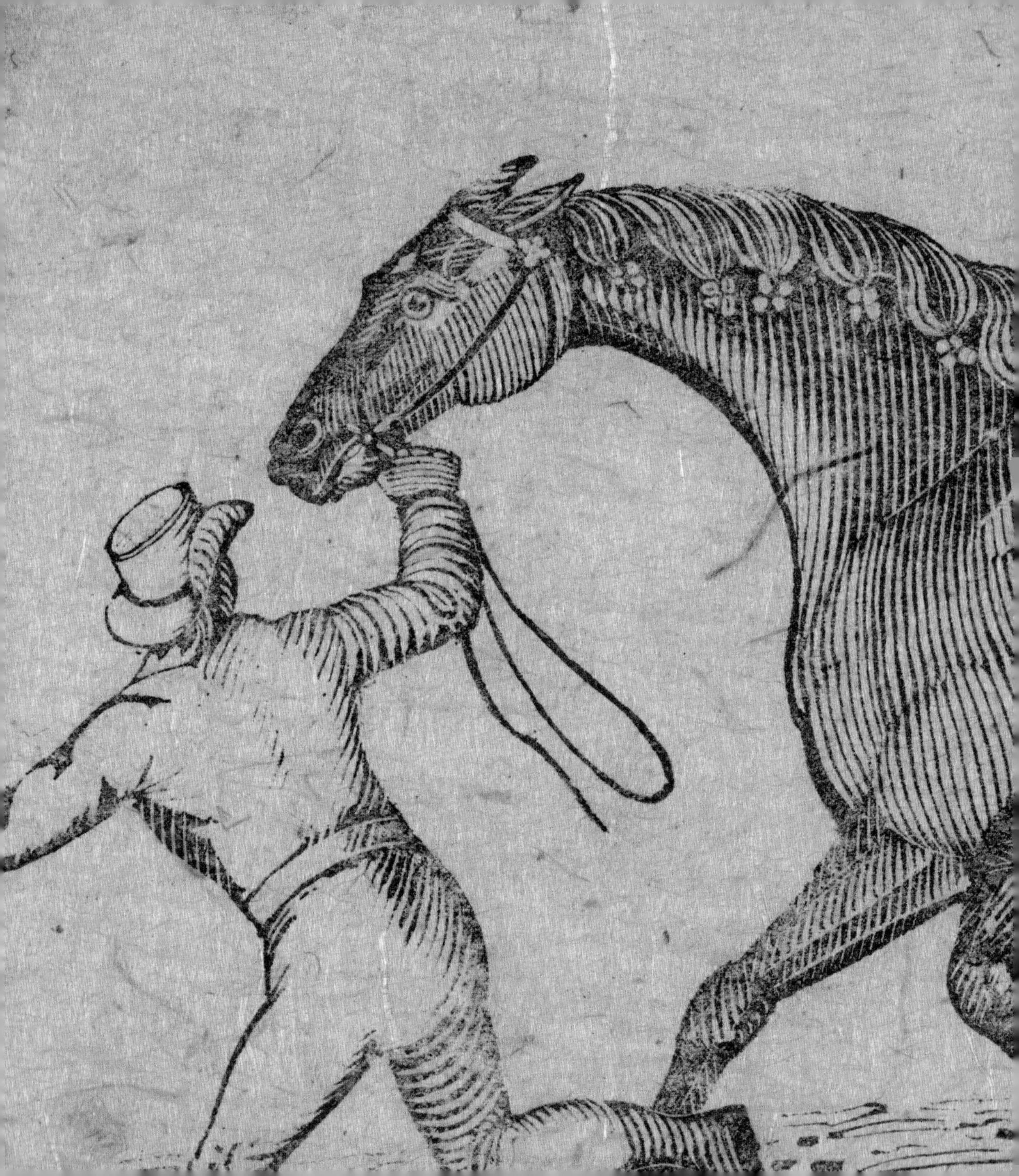

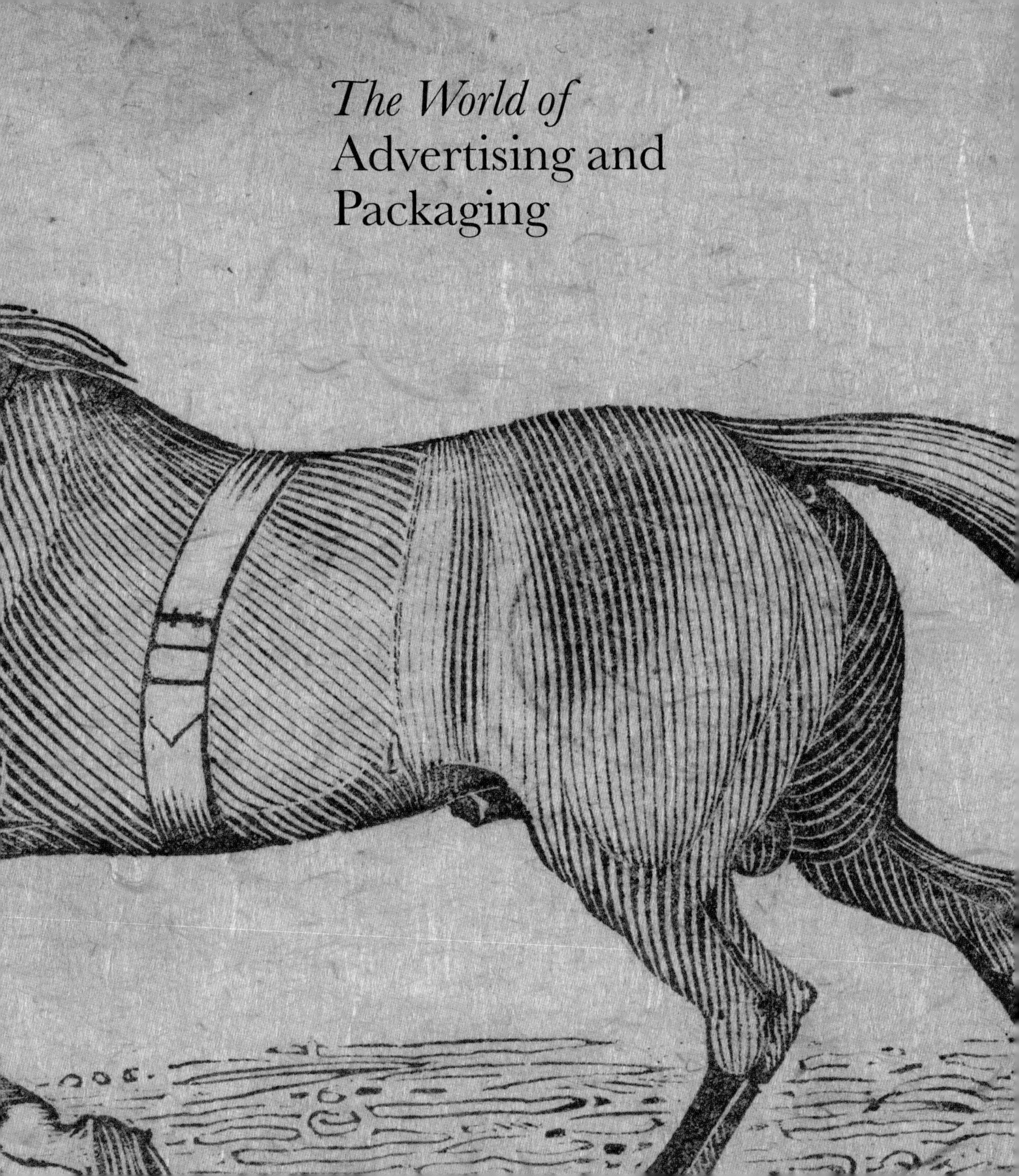
The World of
Advertising and
Packaging

Handbills

Sometimes called flyers, handbills were the advertising medium of choice for small traders and retailers and for peripatetic entrepreneurs without permanent premises (especially entertainers). They were freely handed out in the street or slipped under front doors (and survive to this day, especially for builders, decorators and Chinese takeaways).

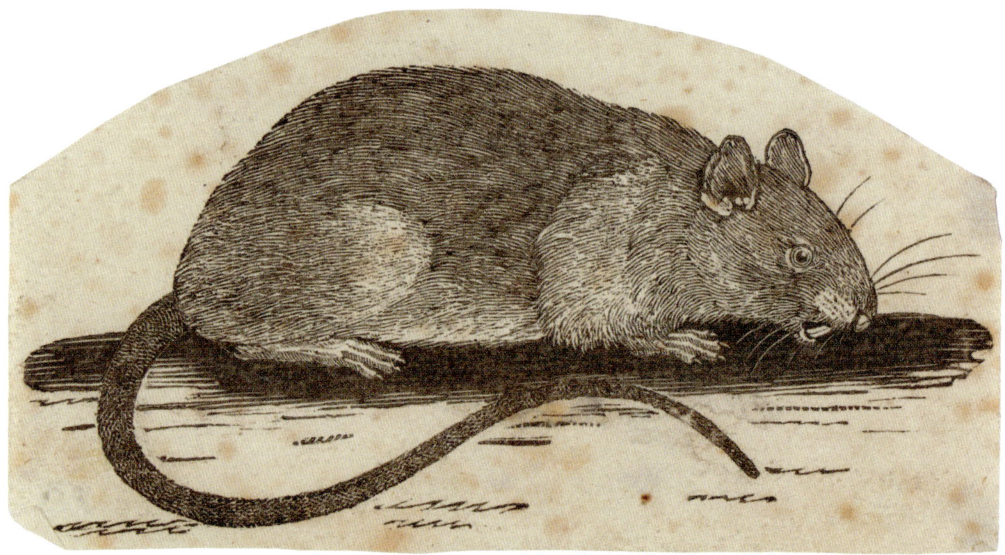

Heading for a handbill advertising rat poison, engraved on wood by Bewick, 9 January 1796, at a charge of 10s. 6d. 60 × 103 mm. British Museum 1882,0311.3732.

Stud notice heading,
engraved on wood by
Bewick, 30 August 1817,
at a charge of 17s. 6d.
57 × 94 mm. British
Museum 1882,0311.4868.

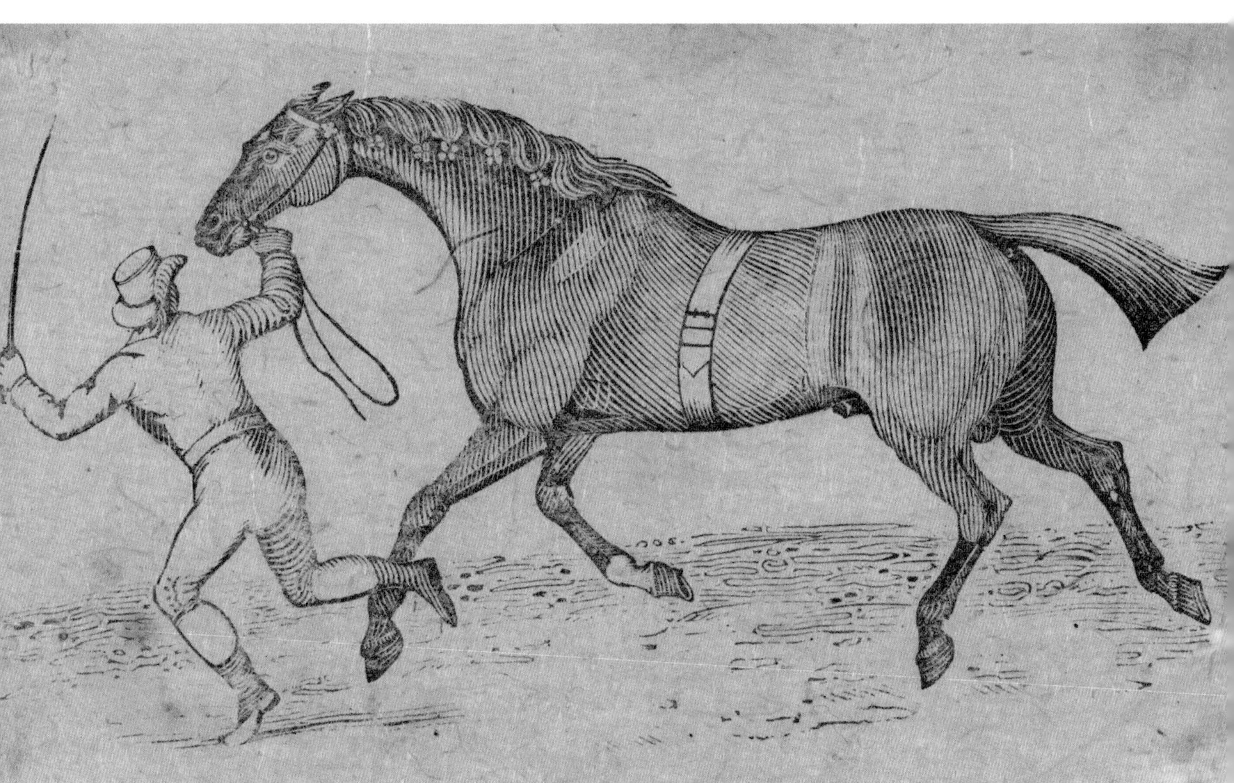

Packaging

In the eighteenth century, most goods, especially foodstuffs, were
sold loose and were neither branded nor pre-packaged but merely
weighed and placed directly in the customer's basket. Granular
and powdery substances such as coffee beans, tea and herbs,
expensive in their own right, required more care and were usually
poured onto squares of paper, some of which were formed into
cones with a twist at the base. (Some traditional fish-and-chip shops
still sell chips in the same way.) It was only a matter of time before
shopkeepers, the majority grocers and apothecaries, realized that
these squares of paper could, when printed, advertise as well as
contain. This practice expanded as erstwhile luxury comestibles
– tea, coffee, chocolate, sugar and tobacco – became objects of
mass consumption by the end of the century. Perhaps because
Bewick was addicted to chewing tobacco, being rarely without
a plug lodged in his lower lip, tobacco papers or labels (now of
great rarity, although tobacco was probably the first commodity
to be sold in printed paper wrappers) outnumber other forms of
packaging in his surviving archive. Many feature a blank area,
indicating that the original woodblock was commissioned by a
local printer (not by a tobacconist or grocer) and fenestrated to
allow for any retailer's name and address to be inserted.

Tobacco cut, engraved on wood by Bewick, *c.* 1775. The medallion shows the traditional American Indian, with a pestle and mortar (for grinding snuff) and a tobacco plant in the background. The medallion is encircled by an Ourobouros, a serpent devouring its tail. This ancient mystical symbol was much favoured by alchemists as representing the guardian of a treasure that could only be gained by destroying it. Presumably it features here because tobacco is usually best enjoyed by setting fire to it. 73 × 55 mm. British Museum 1882,0311.4092.

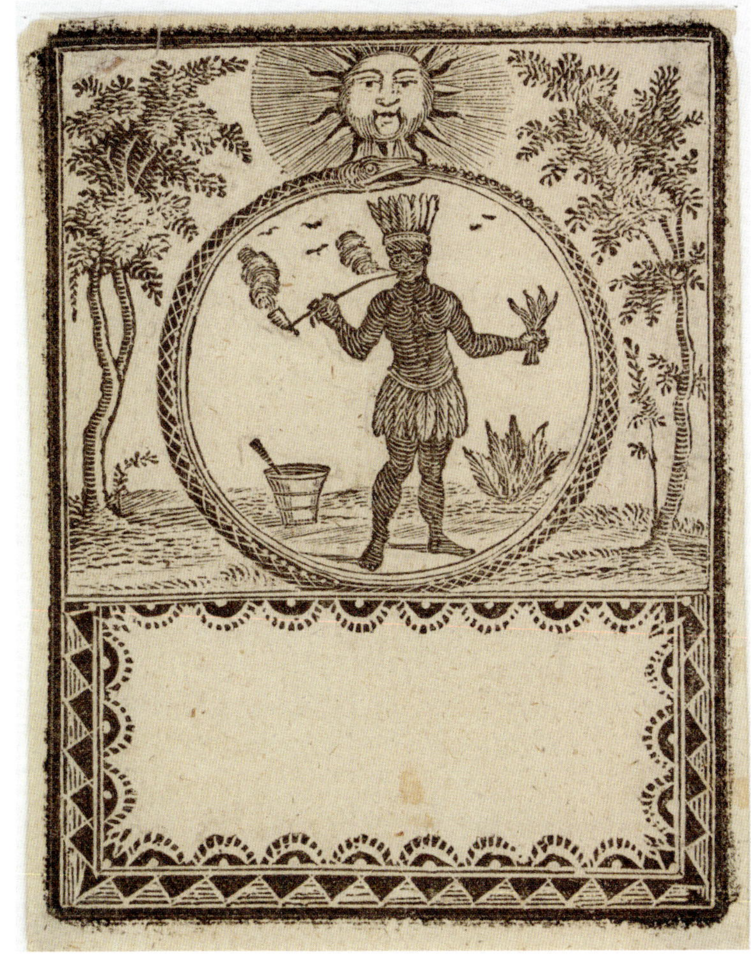

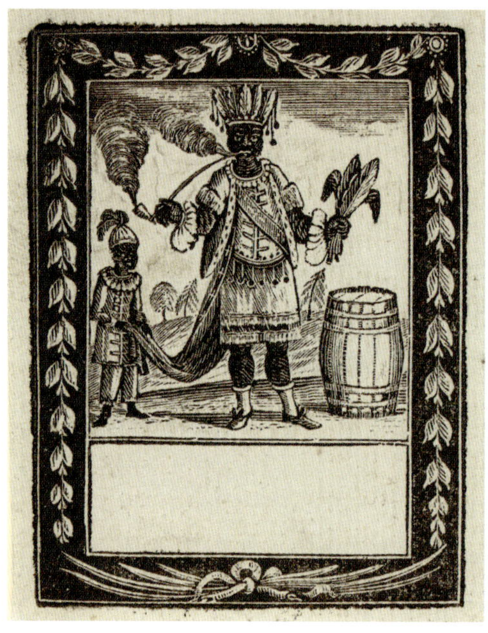 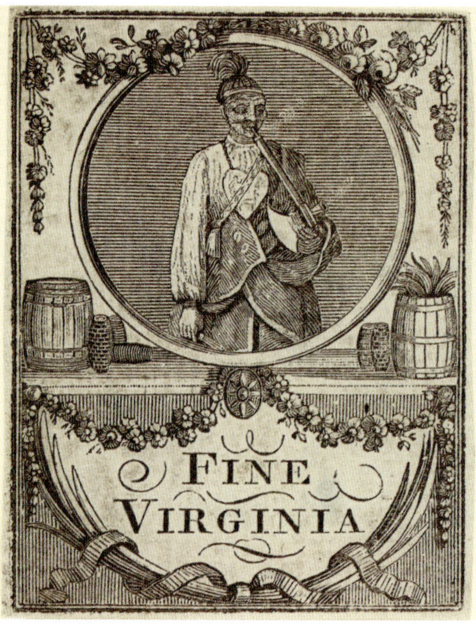

Tobacco cut, engraved on wood by Bewick, *c.* 1777, featuring a border composed of tobacco leaves and the traditional American Indian replaced by an African prince, a subtle acknowledgement that tobacco, like sugar, was harvested and processed by plantation slavery. 77 × 60 mm. British Museum 1882,0311.3227.

Tobacco cut, engraved on wood by Bewick, *c.* 1782, featuring an unusually detailed American Indian warrior (possibly based upon a portrait of Austenaco, one of the three Cherokee emissaries who visited London in 1762) with a traditional scalp lock, a gorget (chest-plate) and a tomahawk-bladed pipe of war. He wears a linen shirt gathered at the wrists and is wrapped in a blanket, both common European trade goods. 77 × 60 mm. British Museum 1882,0311.3228.

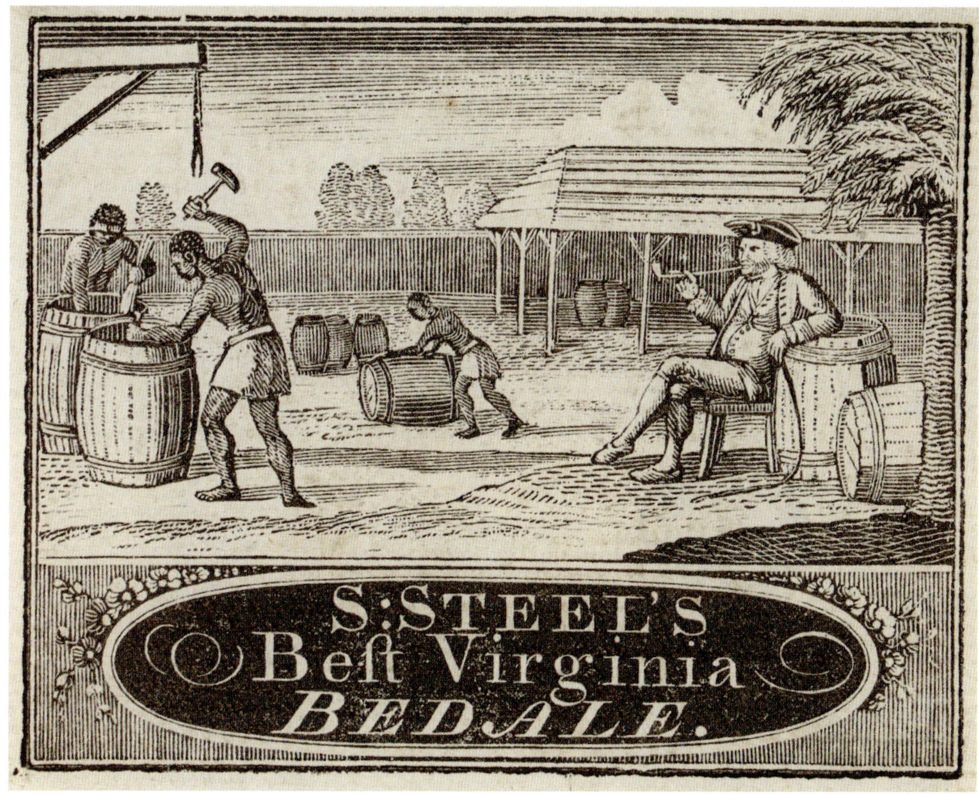

Tobacco cut, engraved on wood by Bewick, *c.* 1781, for Samuel Steel, a wealthy grocer in Bedale, North Yorkshire. The iconography now makes plain that the enjoyment of tobacco is the white man's privilege alone but – unusually – the planter's or overseer's whip emphasizes that the labour involved in its production was coerced. 65 × 75 mm. British Museum 1882,0311.3226.

The World of
Travel

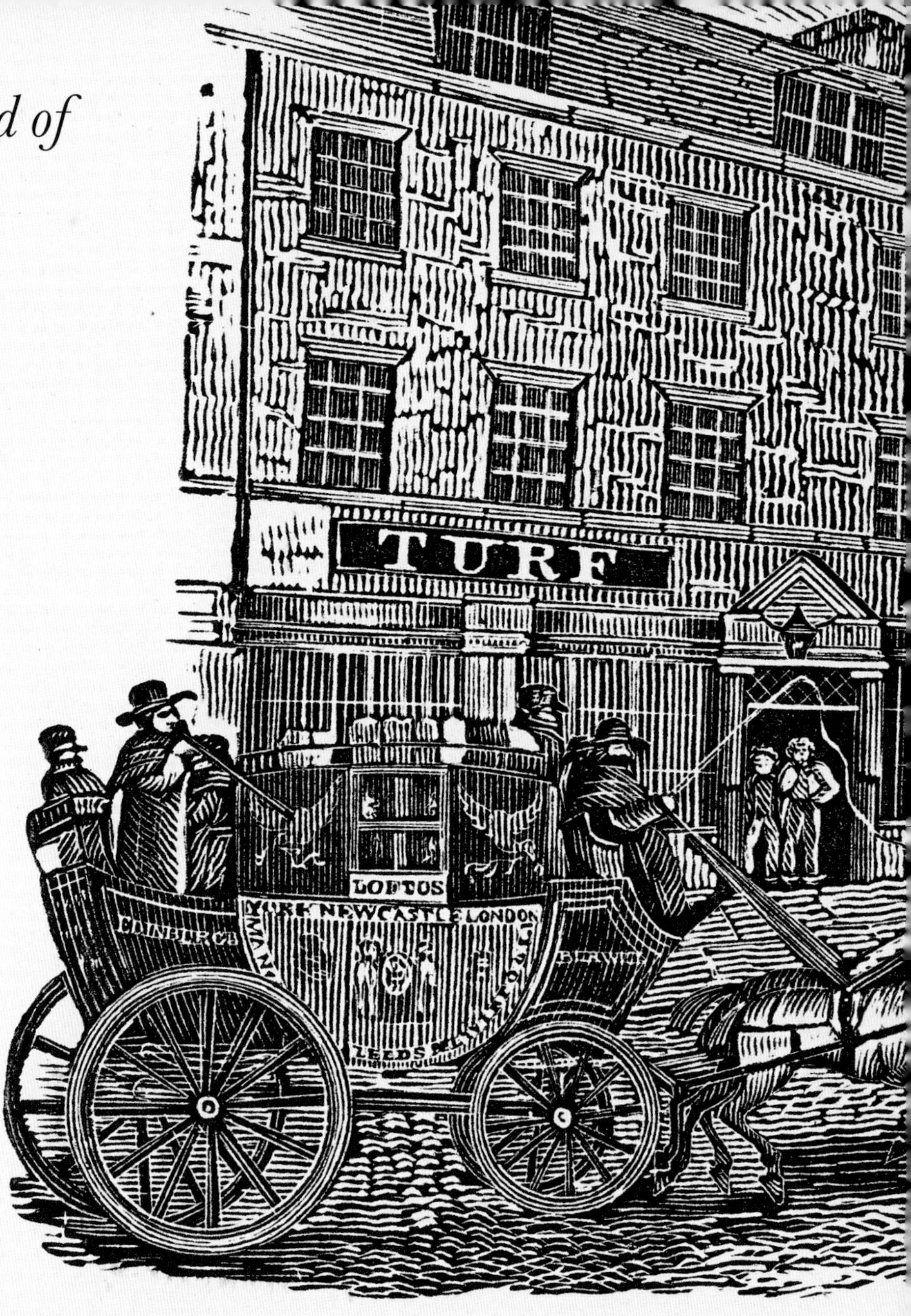

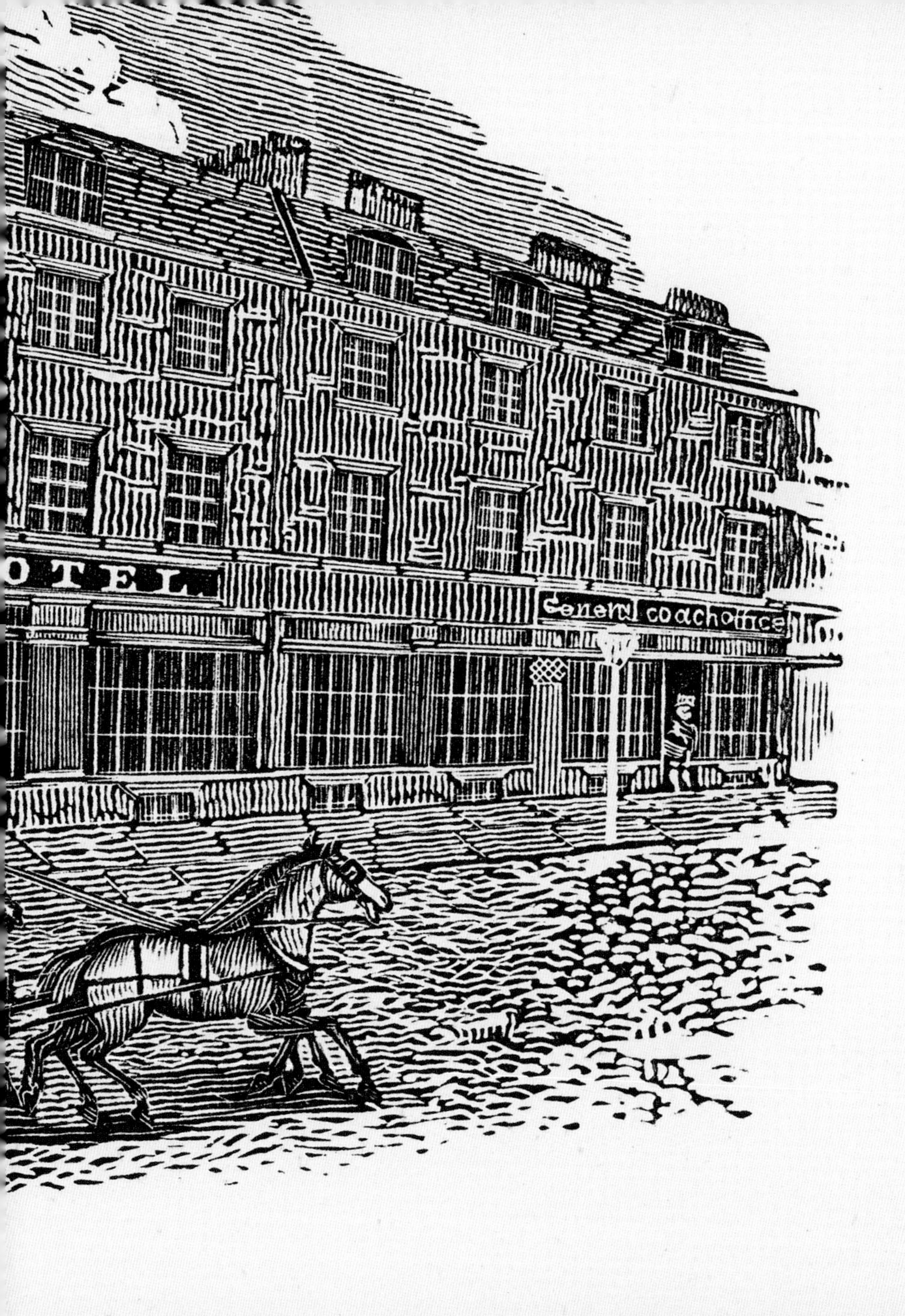

OTEL
General coach office

Although most people tended to live and work in the place of
their birth, it has been estimated that, by the end of the eighteenth
century, one in six of the population had lived, at least for a time,
in London. The majority of them would have been in service,
for when the wealthy moved from the country to the city for the
'season', they brought their retinue of servants with them. Their
numbers were swelled by chapmen, hawkers, itinerant actors,
journeymen in search of work, commercial travellers, men of
business, and circuit and assize judges. Although the roads at
the beginning of the century were often difficult to the point of
impassibility, the turnpike system by the late 1790s had wrought
major improvements, so that by 1825 the Royal Mail coach from
Newcastle took a shade under thirty-six hours to reach London,
three hundred miles to the south.

Modes of transport varied. Many people simply walked.
Others hitched rides on goods waggons, took the stage or mail
coach or hired a post-chaise, according to their pocket. Only
the wealthiest had their own carriages. All travellers, whether
of high or low degree, needed sustenance; along the great trunk
roads coaching inns sprang up. These were often substantial
establishments, catering to the needs of both human and equine
customers. For example, the inns at Hounslow, the first halt from
London to Bath, provided stabling for two thousand horses.

Coaching was a major industry which, by virtue of its timetables
and long before the railways, introduced a standard time across the
kingdom. It also generated a plethora of printed paper including
posting bills, handbills, waybills listing freight or passengers,
timetables, tickets and bills of fare. An illustration to the latter,
though trivial in the scheme of things and casually turned over by
Ralph Beilby to the fourteen-year-old Thomas Bewick, opened
undreamed-of possibilities. As he recalled in his *Memoir* many years
later, 'a cut of the "George & Dragon" for a barr bill [for William
How], attracted so much notice & had so many praises bestowed
upon it, that this kind of work greatly increased upon us, and were
followed by cuts for children's books …'.

Coaching

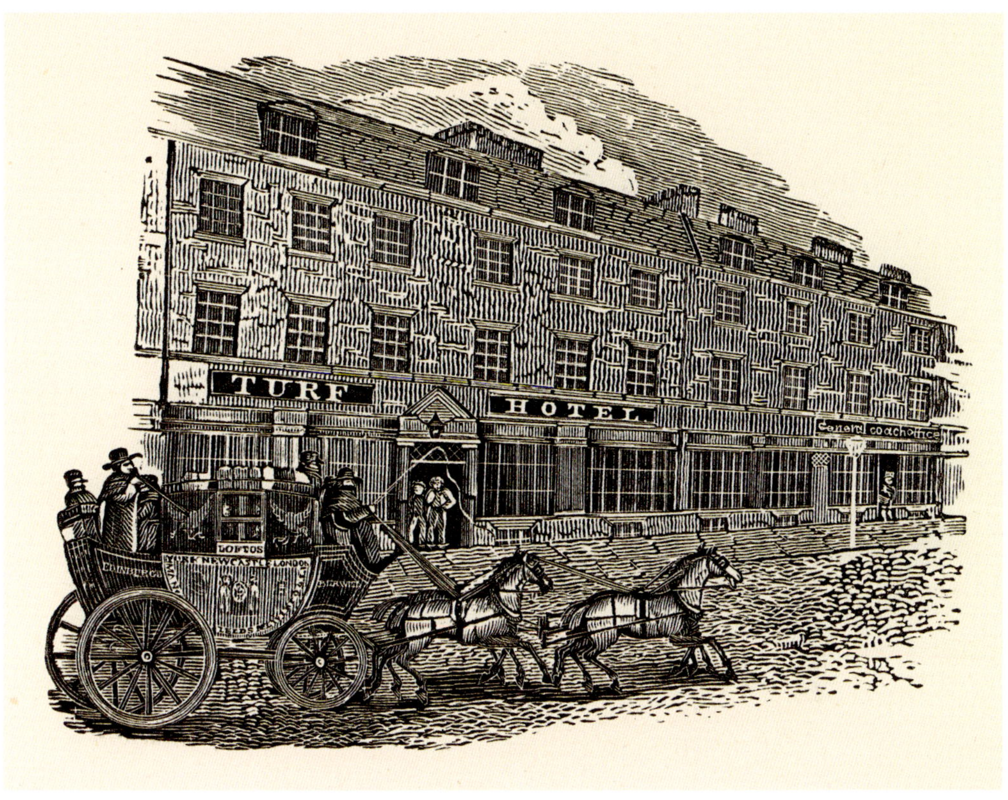

Vignette device for a waybill issued by the General
Coach Office at the Turf Hotel, Newcastle, engraved on
wood by Bewick, 9 July 1825, at a charge of £1 5s. 0d.
William Loftus managed the Office and the vignette
shows the arrival of one of his coaches. 90 × 105 mm.
Private collection.

Poster heading for the Trafalgar Coach, engraved on wood by Bewick,
1 April 1807, at a charge of £6 6s. 0d. Bewick himself has added a few
touches in his own hand to this impression, extending the reins held by the
coachman and – for reasons best known to himself – crossing through the
image of the coach. 140 × 386 mm. British Museum 1882,0311.2808.

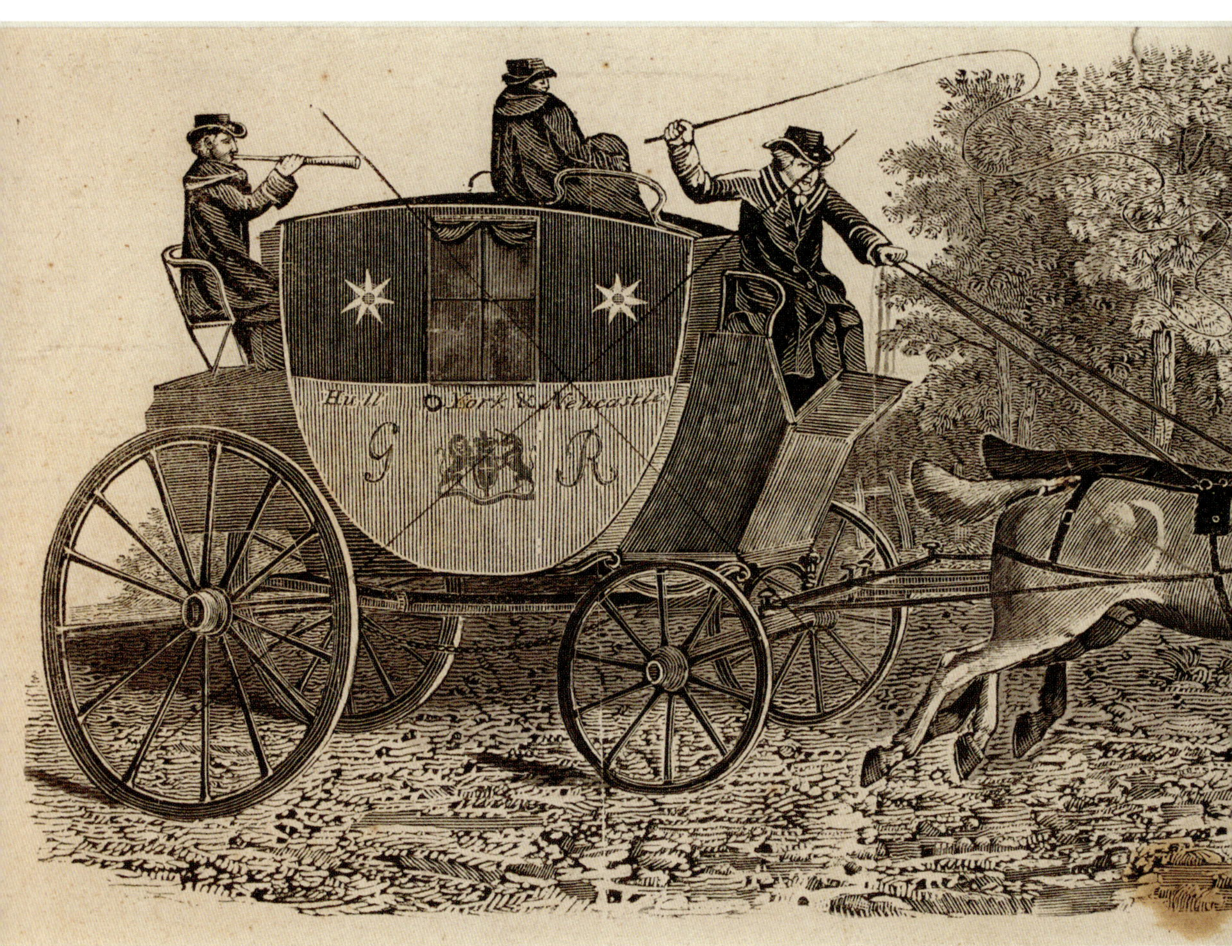

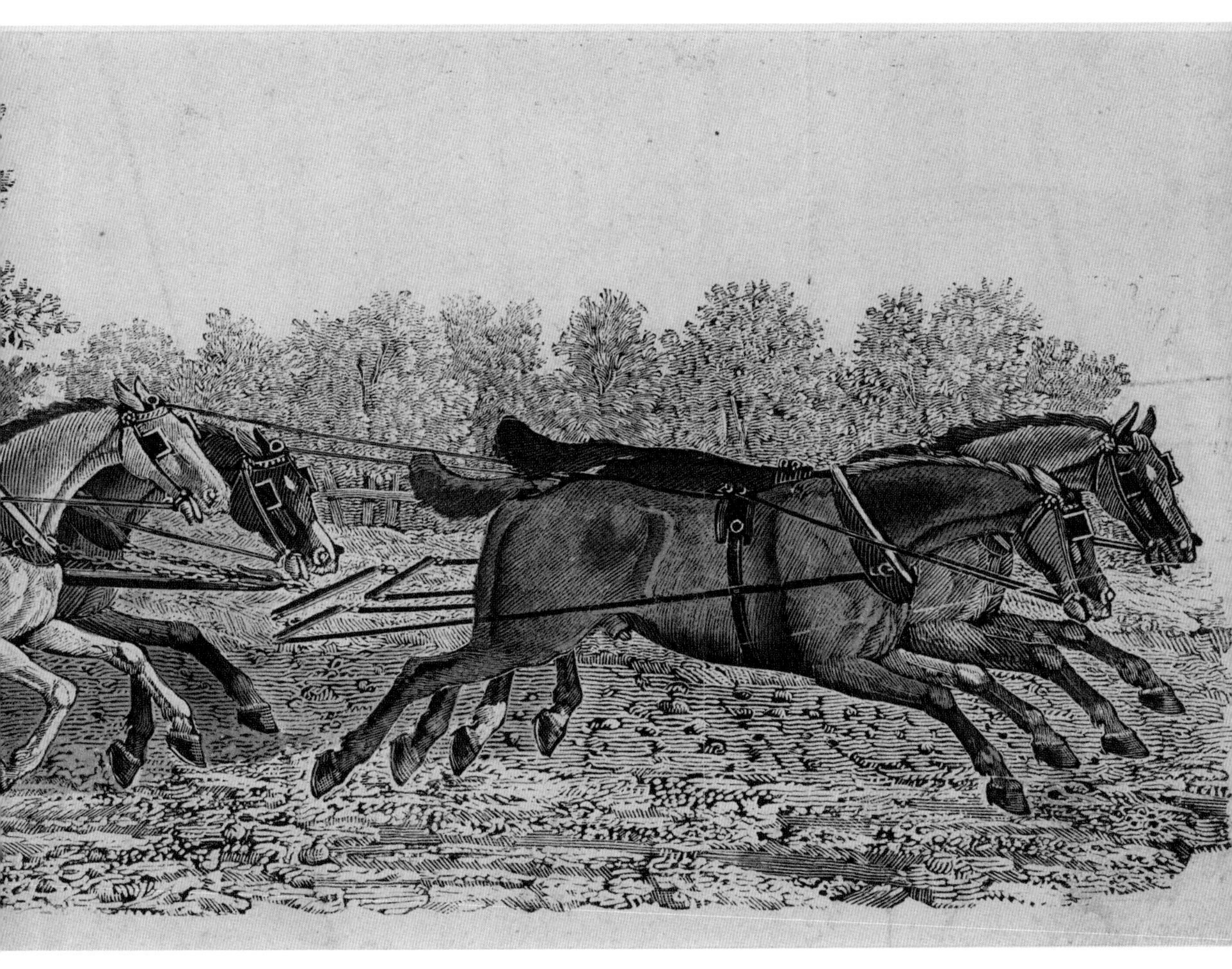

Bills of fare

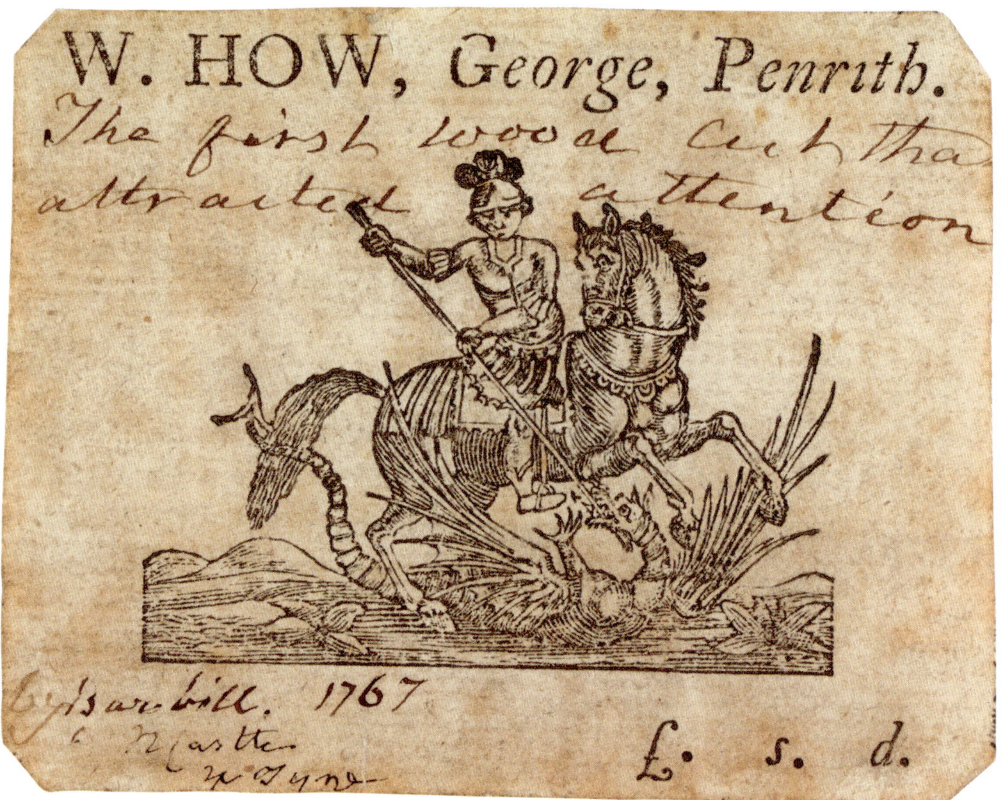

Bill of fare device for William How of the George Inn,
Penrith, engraved on wood by Bewick, 1767. This was
the seed of his career as an illustrator, as indicated
in the inscription by Jane Bewick. 57 × 72 mm. British
Museum 1882,0311.3208.

Bill of fare device for the Cock Inn, Newcastle, engraved on wood by Bewick, *c.* 1775, for innkeeper George Wilson. It was here that Bewick's apprenticeship indentures were signed. The same block was used by Matthew Hall when advertising in the *Newcastle Chronicle*, 28 April 1781, that he had taken over the Cock Inn, indicating how a woodblock could fulfil more than one function. 45 × 55 mm. British Museum 1882,0311.3214.

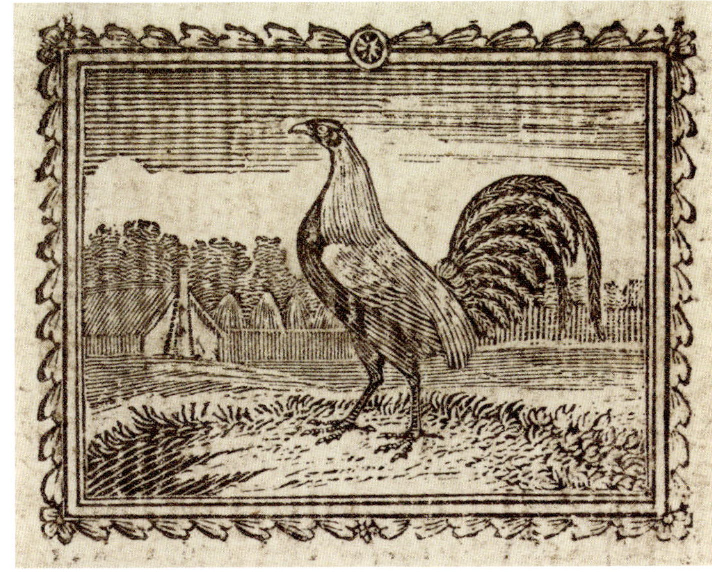

Bill of fare device for the Black Bull at Wooler, engraved on wood by Bewick, 25 May 1778, at a charge of 2s. 6d. 40 × 45 mm. British Museum 1882,0311.3211.

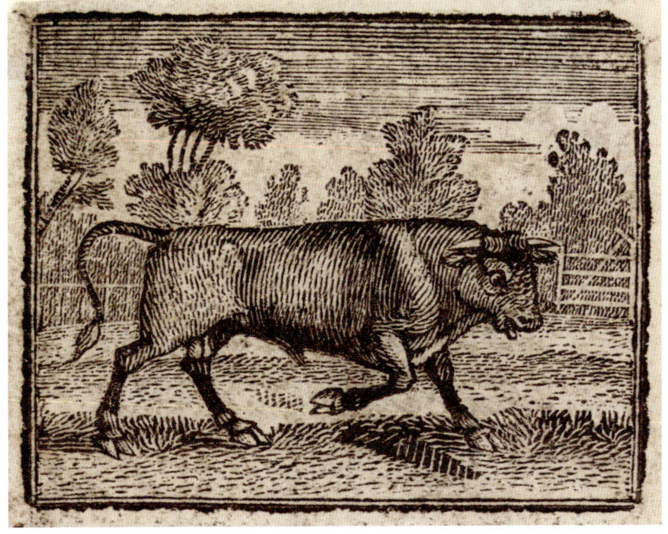

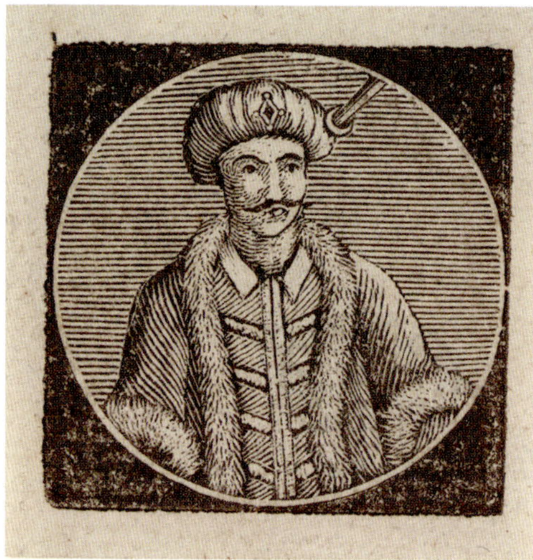

Bill of fare device for the Turk's Head, Newcastle, engraved on wood by Bewick, 9 December 1779, at a charge of 5s. One of the most prominent inns of the town, the Turk's Head was renowned for its cockfighting pit. 40 × 40 mm. British Museum 1882,0311.3213.

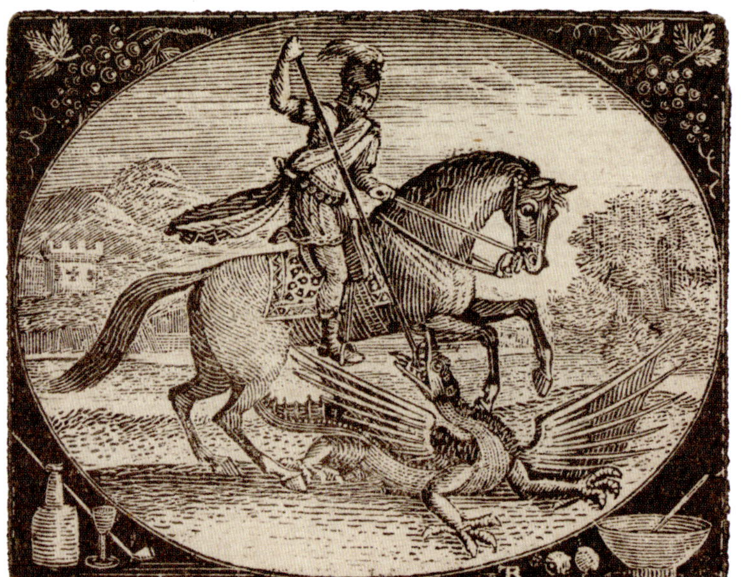

Bill of fare device for the George Inn, Penrith, engraved on wood by Bewick, 19 February 1780, at a charge of 12s. The border to the cut is decorated with all the accoutrements of good cheer, including grapes, a pipe of tobacco, a punch bowl and a bottle of wine. 58 × 70 mm. British Museum 1882,0311.3209.

Bill of fare for the Crown and Thistle Inn, Newcastle, an establishment 'much frequented by commercial gentlemen'. This coaching inn was taken over by Henry Sunderland on 1 September 1792 and the bill was engraved on copper in the Bewick workshop, 13 October 1792 at a charge of £1 17s. 6d. 180 × 105 mm. Private collection.

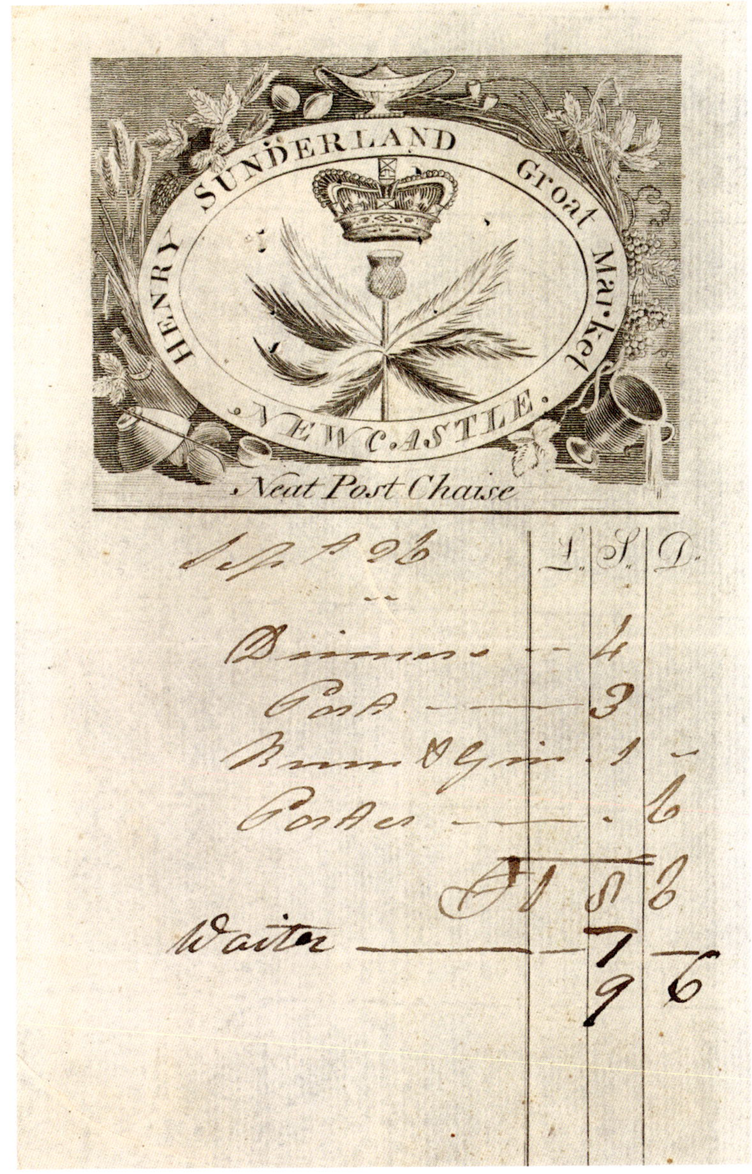

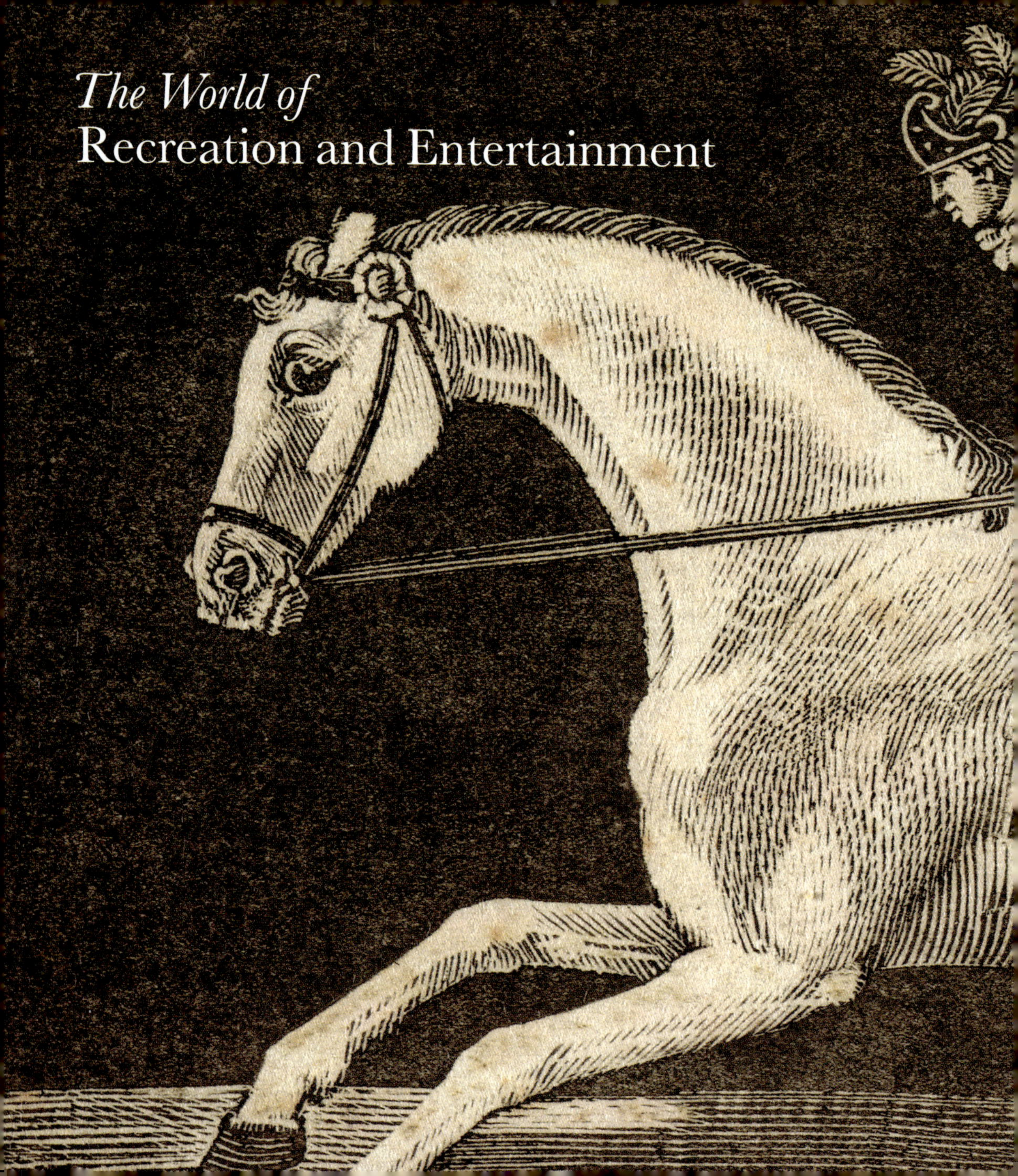
The World of
Recreation and Entertainment

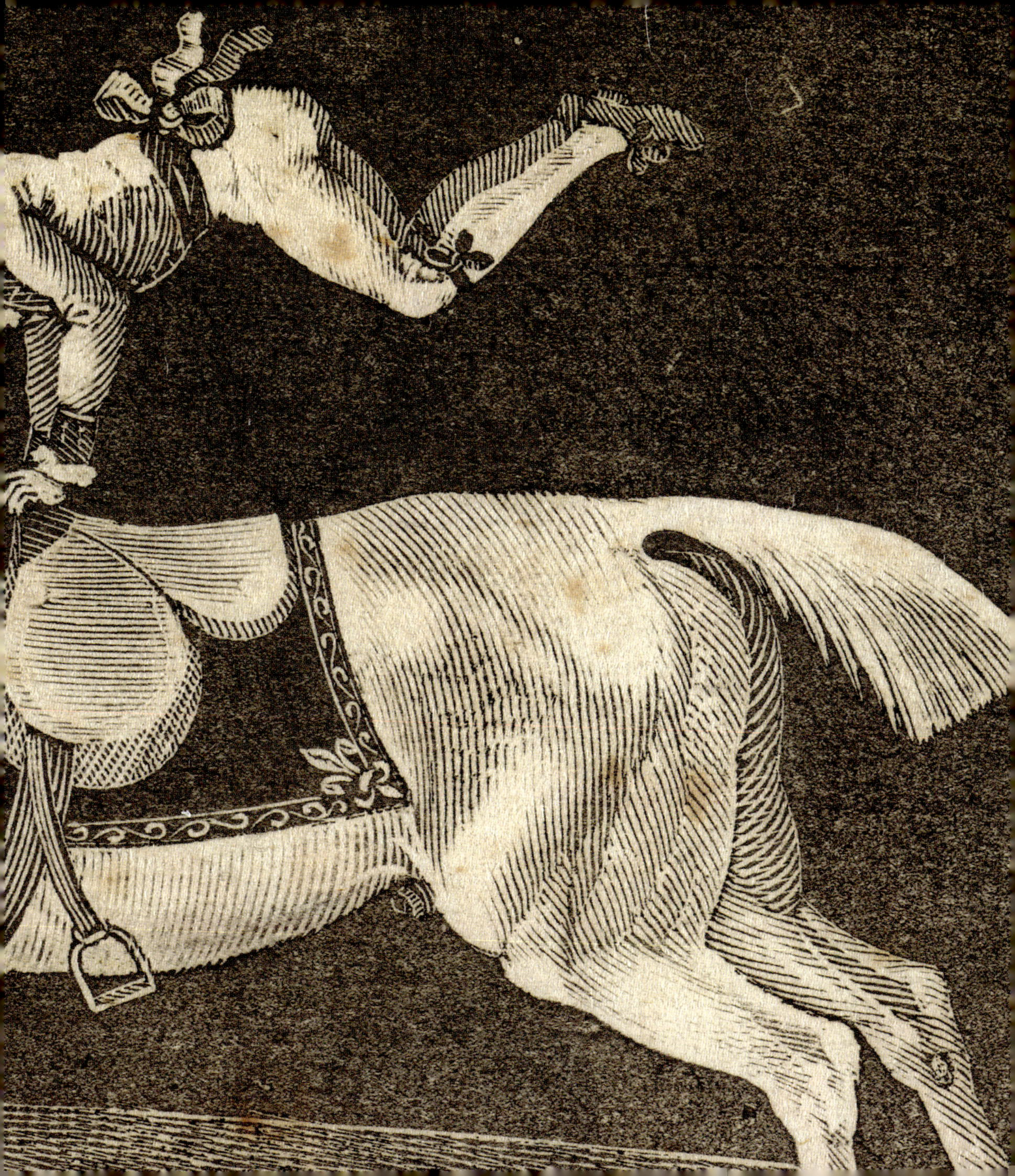

Recreation

Whilst life in the country was largely determined by the seasons, by the vagaries of the weather and the hours of daylight, life in English industrial cities in the later eighteenth century was transformed by managerial demands for ever-increasing productivity. This phenomenon has caused some commentators to call the Industrial Revolution the 'Industrious Revolution', as the period between 1750 and 1800 saw the disappearance of many public and religious holidays, the elimination of St Monday (which workers had traditionally claimed as part of the weekend), the introduction of a six-day working week, and a working day which now extended for at least twelve hours and often considerably more. Against such losses of privilege, how did workers (anyone from an unskilled labourer to a journeyman, a shopkeeper or a master of a small workshop) let off steam?

Certainly, a warm welcome awaited such men at the local tavern, where they could 'wet their clay' on payday, and many indeed sought oblivion in alcohol. Others used the tavern's facilities (which frequently included libraries and the latest newspapers) to gather as more or less formal societies, partly convivial, partly educational, partly political or philosophical, but invariably fuelled by heroic quantities of punch. Bewick was a member of several, from Swarley's Club at the Black Boy (mostly consisting of 'Merchants or respectable Tradesmen' and which was closed down by government spies) to a loose affiliation of 'Tradesmen, Banker's Clerks, Artizans & Agents of various kinds', whom he described as 'staunch advocates for the liberties of Mankind', who met nearly every evening at the Blue Bell and its newsroom. (Women appear to have had no such refuges.) Newcastle numbered well over fifty such clubs, including benefit societies for specific trades (such as tobacconists), freemasons' lodges, floral societies and debating clubs, and some – the Free and Easy Johns for example, whose name suggested a delight in unfettered drinking, smoking and bawdy ballads (as was undoubtedly the case) – also embodied a more serious role as mutually beneficial societies for members in distress. The wealthy needed no such clubs. To all intents and purposes, they already had them in the council chamber of the Corporation and the boardrooms of their banks and insurance offices.

Sport enjoyed an immense popularity at all levels of society but, the racecourse apart, these were invariably blood sports, pitting gamecocks against one another, coursing for hares and hunting for foxes. Betting was the spur to the first two activities (the Georgians loved a wager), bloodletting the incentive to the latter. Attitudes did not start to change until the fledgling cult of sensibility achieved a more widespread influence in the nineteenth century.

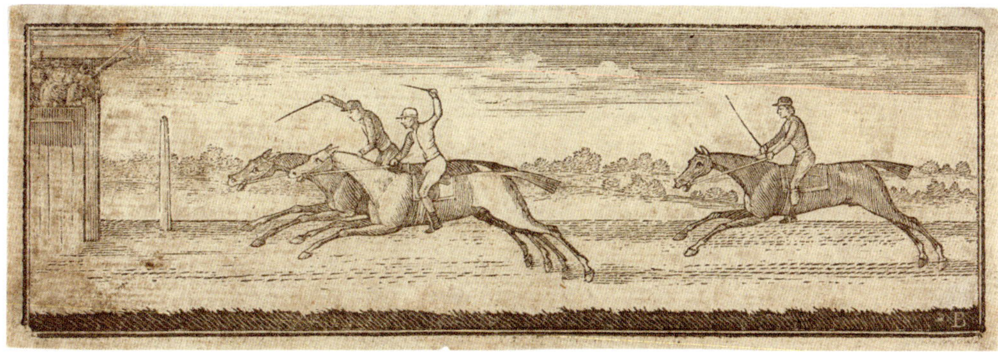

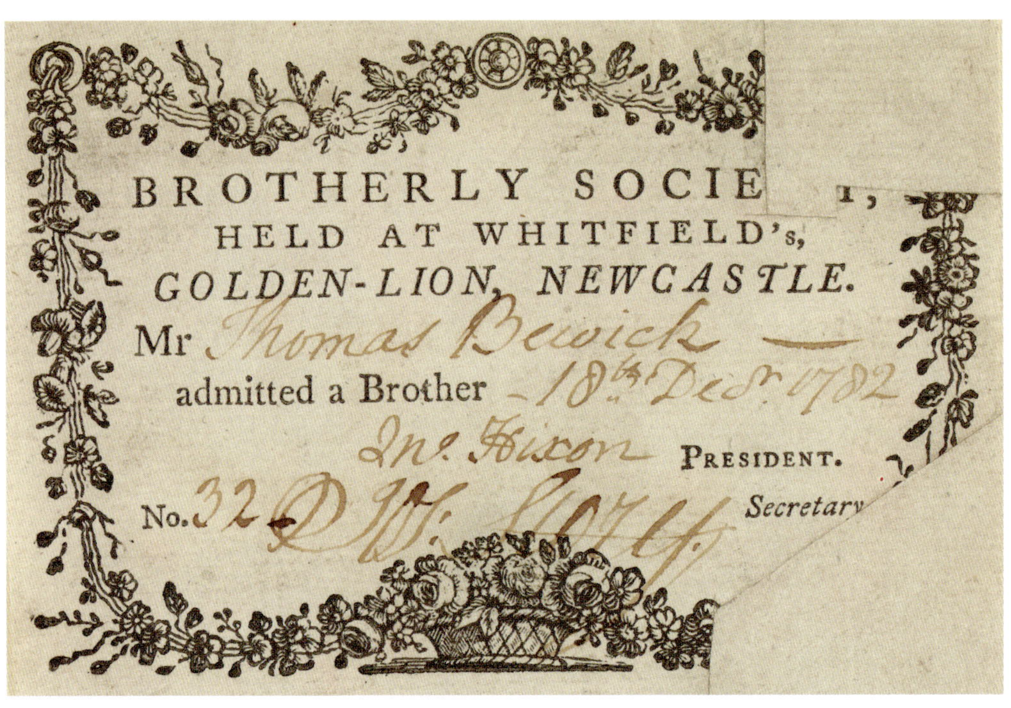

Membership card admitting Thomas Bewick,
18 December 1782, as the thirty-second member of the
Brotherly Society held at Matthew Whitfield's Golden
Lion Inn. The floral device was possibly the 'Border on
Wood for Cards' for printer Thomas Angus, engraved
by Bewick, 29 November 1780, at a charge of 10s. 6d.
70 × 100 mm. British Museum 1882,0311.2416.

'Ticket Plate' for Lodge 12 of the Free and Easy Johns at Lemington, near Newcastle. Engraved on copper by Robert Bewick (a copy of an earlier plate engraved by his father Thomas in 1787), 17 May 1817, at a charge of £1 11s. 6d. 100 × 68 mm. British Museum 1882,0311.3146.

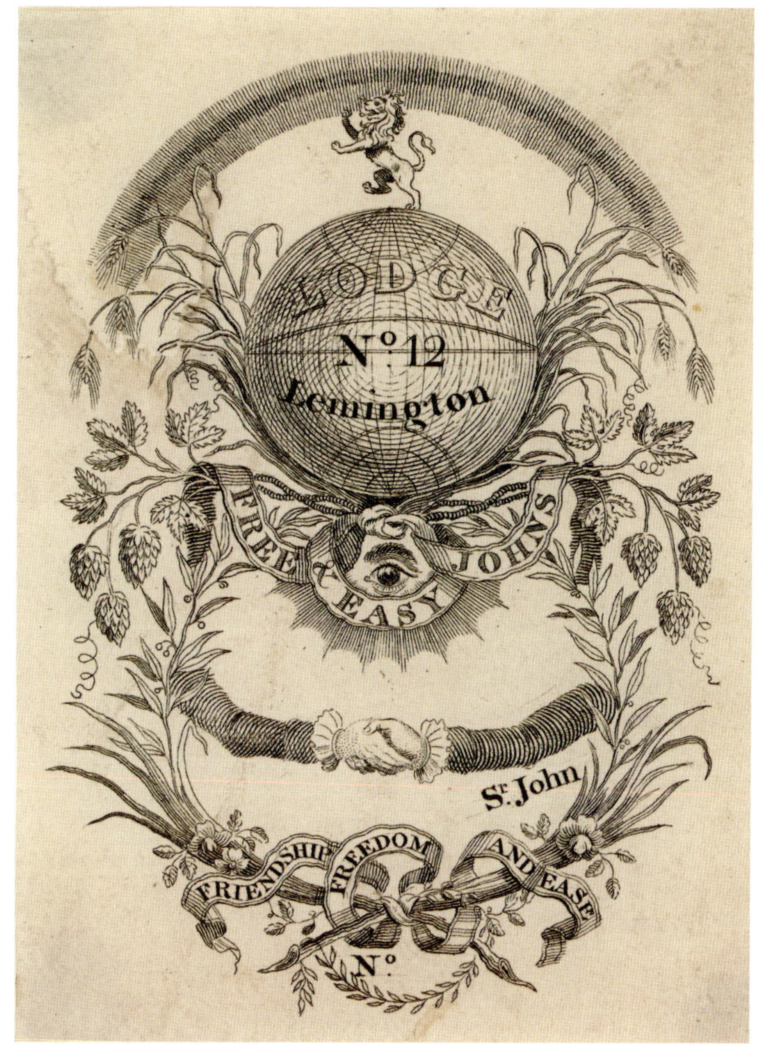

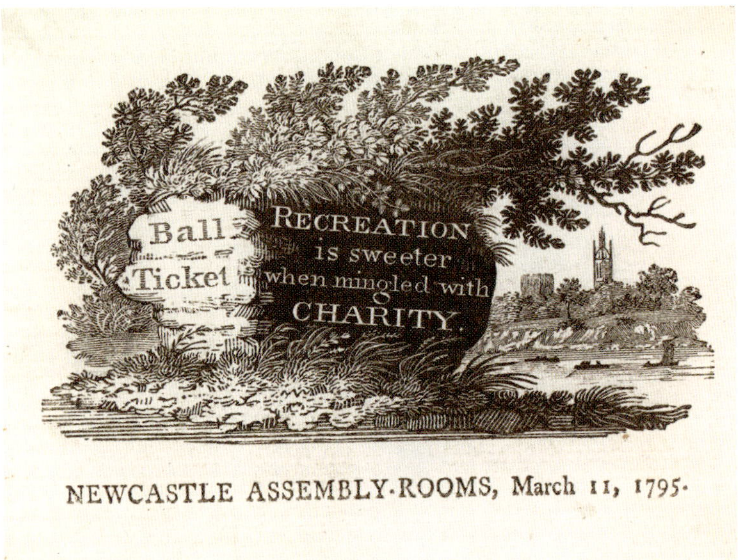

Ball ticket of admission, engraved on wood by Bewick, 7 March 1795, at a charge of 15s. Commissioned and settled by the industrialist Isaac Cookson (as an act of charity). The Newcastle newspapers reported that the tickets cost 5s. 6d. each and that the proprietors would allow the Assembly Rooms to be used without charge. 'After payment of lights, music and all incidental expenses', the surplus would be 'applied to the relief of the Poor at this severe season'. 75 × 100 mm. British Museum 1882,0311.3739.

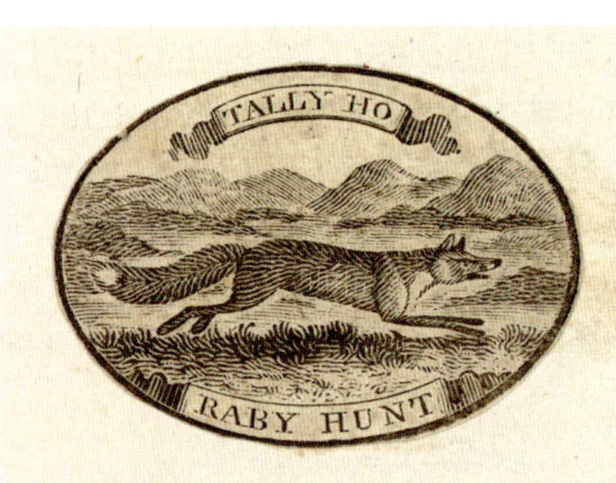

Device for a hunt card, engraved on wood by Bewick for the Richmond printer Robert Coatsworth, 25 October 1794, at a charge of 10s. 6d. The Raby Hunt was established by William Henry Vane, third earl of Darlington, a passionate devotee of the sport, who kept hounds at Raby Castle for half a century and hunted a stretch of land from south Yorkshire to Northumberland. Buttons and uniforms (black jackets with golden, fox-crested collars) for the Hunt generated much work for the tailors of the area and the regular meetings of the 'Gentlemen of the Raby Hunt' doubtless delighted proprietors of the local hostelries. 30 × 40 mm. Private collection.

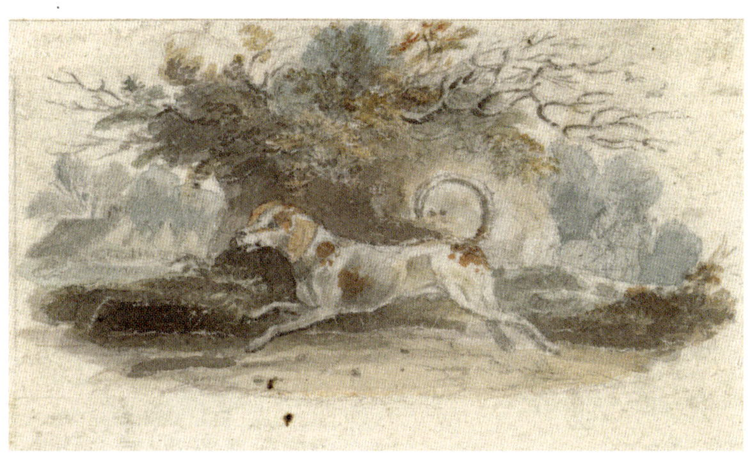

Hunt card for Matthew Culley's beagles, pencil and watercolour study by Bewick for the etching and engraving on copper by his son Robert, 23 December 1815, charged at £1 11s. 6d. Beagles were employed to hunt hares and were followed on foot. By the mid-eighteenth century, beagling had dwindled to the status of a quaint relic, unable to compete with the dash and danger of foxhunting. Culley's pack may have been a conscious attempt to revive the practice.

45 × 60 mm, British Museum 1882,0311.1390 (study);
92 × 63 mm, private collection (hunt card).

Entertainment

Although many during the Regency period would deny it, everyone was up for a show. Thanks to concessionary rates offered by showmen, typically 'Ladies & Gentlemen 1s., Tradesmen 6d., Servants 3d.', this was where farm workers, butchers, serving wenches and apprentices rubbed shoulders with the 'middling' classes and the wealthy. Social distinctions crumbled when curiosity was piqued, and few discriminated between 'low' (popular) and 'high' (classical) entertainment, to the despair of more sensitive souls such as William Wordsworth. He railed against Bartholomew Fair and its ilk, where 'all out-o'-th'-way, far-fetch'd, perverted things / Of Man' were all 'jumbled up together to make up / This Parliament of Monsters.'

Certainly Newcastle, especially during Race and Assize weeks, had its share of delegates to this 'Parliament'. Albinos abounded, as did dwarfs, giants, fire-proof ladies, 'Spotted Boys', stone-eaters (their meals could be heard chinking in their stomachs 'as if in a Pocket'), double-headed heifers and sagacious animals of all sorts. Some entertainers brought a measure of learning with them. Appearing as a performer with Bannister and West's circus in the North East in 1810, the 'celebrated Patagonian Sampson', Giovanni Battista Belzoni (later renowned as an explorer of Egyptian antiquities and occasionally claimed as the model for Indiana Jones), not only displayed his stupendous feats of strength but also exhibited 'Hydraulic Experiments on the Power of Water'.

Aided by the improved road network, shows could travel vast distances. Pidcock's 'Grand Menagerie' visited Newcastle as part of an itinerary that stretched from London via York to Edinburgh and Glasgow. When preparing his *General History of Quadrupeds* and whilst revising later editions, Bewick found such displays invaluable and forged close links with their proprietors. Of all the diversions, perhaps the circus was the most popular. It was not the circus as we know it today – although clowns played a major part in its success – but essentially a show of equitation in which riders and their mounts displayed 'Horsemanship in all its Various Departments' whilst thundering around a ring. (In their spare time, the performers acted as riding instructors, a profitable sideline.) Such was their popularity that in 1789 a 'Circus or Amphitheatre' was constructed in an area called the Forth (close to Bewick's home) and rented out to visiting companies of horsemen.

With the opening of permanent theatres in the area (especially Newcastle's Theatre Royal in 1788), the incidence of strolling players setting up in the public rooms of local taverns declined, although such rooms remained popular with many itinerant showmen. Theatre managers tried hard to create an air of decorum and persuade their public towards more classical fare, but

Heading for a handbill, engraved on wood by Bewick, c. 1780, showing an equilibrist and juggler, possibly Rosoman Wilkinson, performing on the slack-rope. Her exotic costume owes its inspiration to Mahomet Achmed Vizaro Mussulmo, an equilibrist who claimed to be Turkish and performed in Arab regalia in London in 1747. Signifying luxury and sensuality, the outfit nevertheless provided a female performer with a loose, free-flowing covering which would neither constrain her movements nor compromise her modesty. 110 × 145 mm. Private collection.

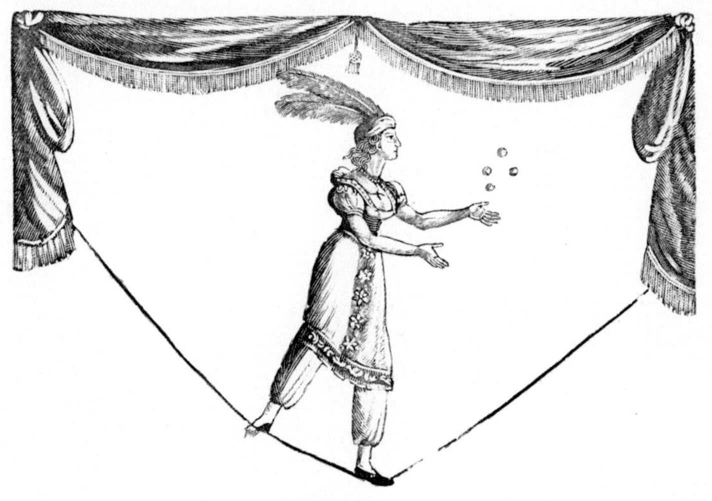

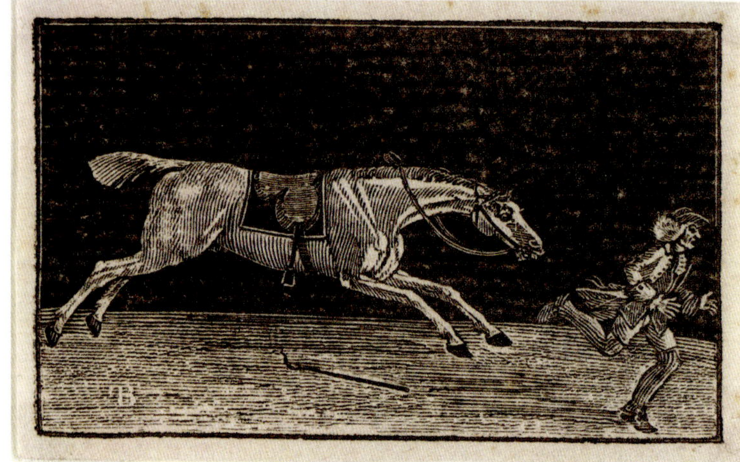

Illustration for a handbill (and benefit night ticket), engraved on wood by Bewick for Mr Humphreys of the Forth Circus, 5 December 1789, at a charge of 7s. 6d. Humphreys was an accomplished horseman and clown whose uproarious performance in 'The Taylor's Ride to Brentford' (in which he is finally chased from the ring by his mount) always brought the house down. 43 × 70 mm. British Museum, 1882,0311.3182.

the audience was not easily weaned from a diet of music, spectacle and acrobatics. A typical bill for the Theatre Royal in 1815 lists 'Sieur Sanches' displaying his 'Antipodean Powers' by walking on the ceiling, followed by the young William Macready and a full supporting cast in Shakespeare's *Othello*, then Sanches singing whilst accompanying himself on the guitar, Sanches performing acrobatics on the slack-rope, and finally a performance of *The Forest of Bondy*, a sentimental melodrama. The cheapest ticket cost a shilling, good value for a performance lasting well over five hours.

Advertising was key to the success of any entertainment and showmen were masters in 'billing the town'; distributing handbills, pasting up posters and inserting details of their offerings in the local newspapers, either as anonymous puffs or as proper notices and frequently as both. This ephemeral material, usually printed upon coarse, poor quality paper, demanded strong, graphic images for which woodcuts (which, depending on their size, could appear in both newspapers and handbills) were ideally suited. Consequently, as with so much else, the world of entertainment beat a path to Bewick's door.

Heading for a handbill, engraved on wood by Bewick for Thomas Denton's 'Grand Mechanical Exhibition', 27 May 1786, at a charge of 10s. 6d. The 'Automaton Writer' was 'so curiously constructed as to be able to write whatever is proposed to it, with Pen and Ink'. 75 × 112 mm. British Museum 1882,0311.4148.

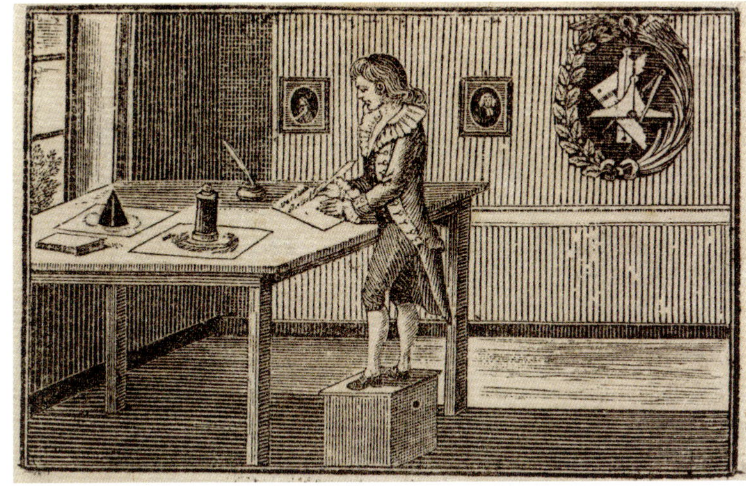

Heading for a handbill, engraved on wood by Bewick for Denton, 27 May 1786, at a charge of 10s. 6d. The 'Speaking Figure' was said to answer all questions in most European languages. Denton's ingenuity could not save him from the gallows, for he was eventually hanged for manufacturing fake coins. 75 × 112 mm. British Museum 1882,0311.4149.

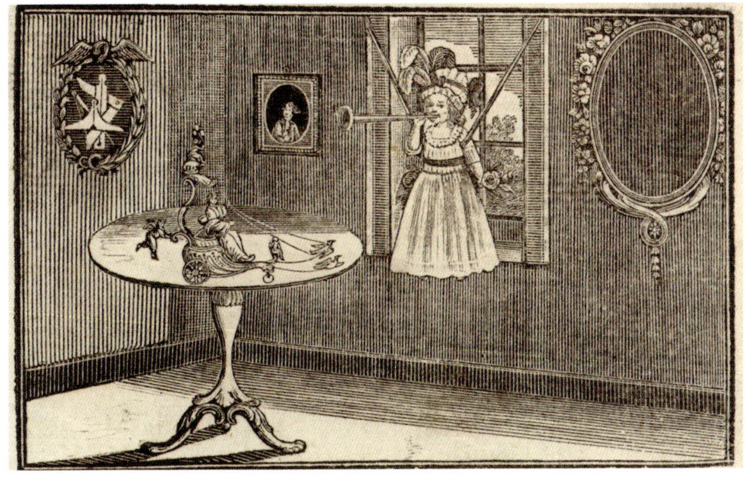

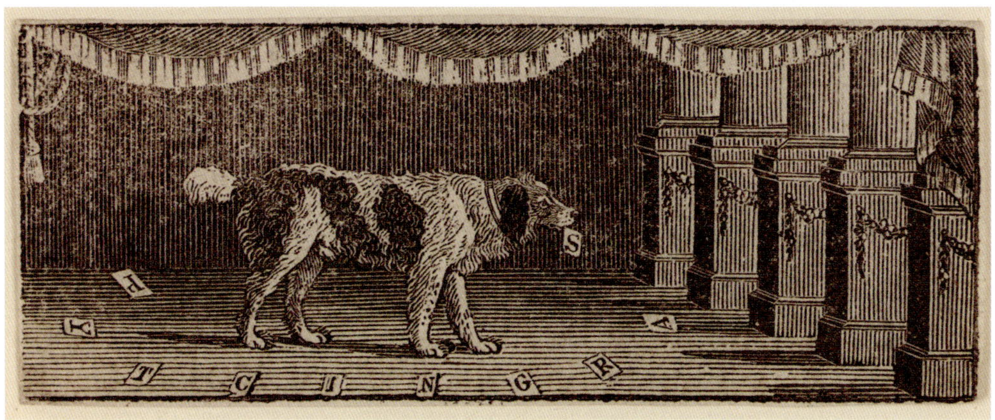

Illustration for a handbill, engraved on wood by Bewick
in 1786, for Frederick Wilkinson's 'Learned English Dog'.
Wilkinson was a multi-talented performer who not only
trained animals to perform tricks but also displayed
feats of horsemanship, acrobatics and rope dancing,
and played on the musical glasses (not all at the same
time). His troupe of entertainers, including daughter
Rosoman, frequently visited Newcastle. 40 × 96 mm.
British Museum 1882,0311.2419.

Illustration for a hand or posting bill, engraved by Bewick on type metal for William Parker of Jones and Parker's Circus, 1 August 1788, at a charge of 12s. It depicts Parker's 'Broad Sword' display, 'with a fierce and vigorous Charge, as in real Action, upon the Spanish Charger'. 245 × 145 mm. British Museum 1882,0311.3184.

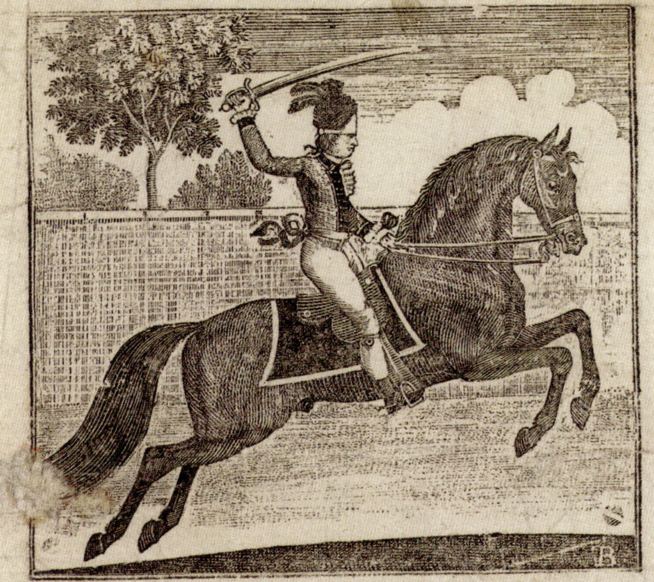

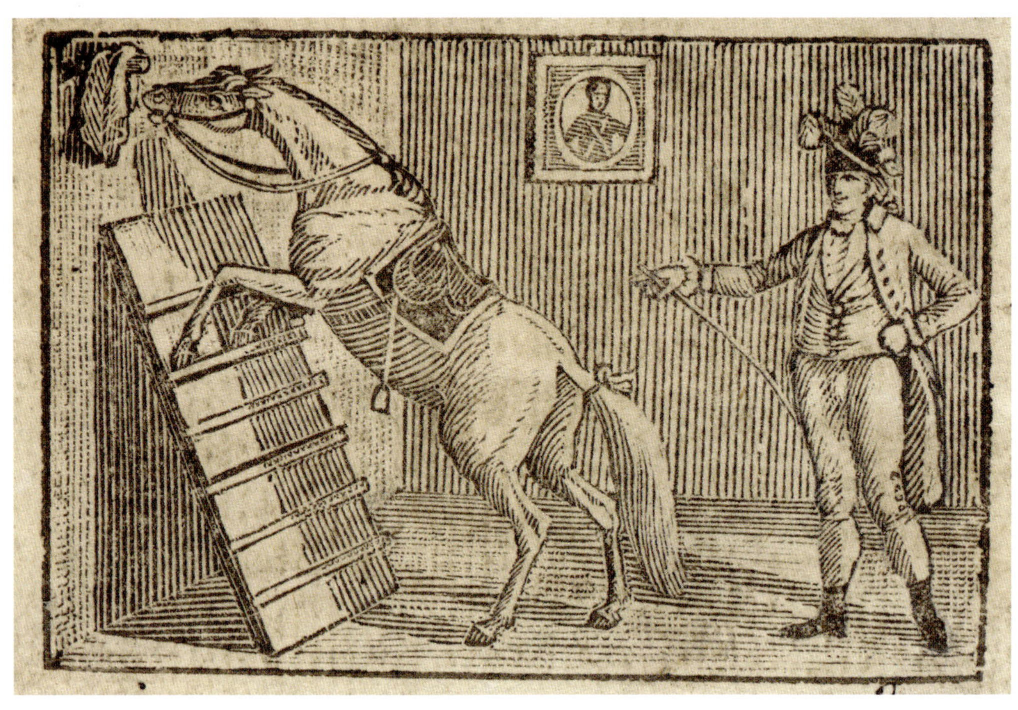

Illustration for a handbill,
engraved on wood by
Bewick, *c.* 1789, for 'The
Sagacious Horse', trained
by Jones and Parker.
48 × 66 mm. British
Museum 1882,0311.3179.

Benefit night ticket, original pen and wash study by Bewick for an engraving on wood, probably executed on 5 December 1789, at a charge of 15s. John Bill Ricketts was the most accomplished equestrian of his generation and in 1793 took the concept of the circus to America. For the evening of 2 January 1790 (delayed because of severe weather) it was announced that he would 'leap from two Horses through a Hogshead suspended in the Air, and recover his situation, the Horses being, at the same time, in full speed'. The manuscript additions are by Jane Bewick following her father's death. 100 × 65 mm. British Museum 1882,0311.1643.

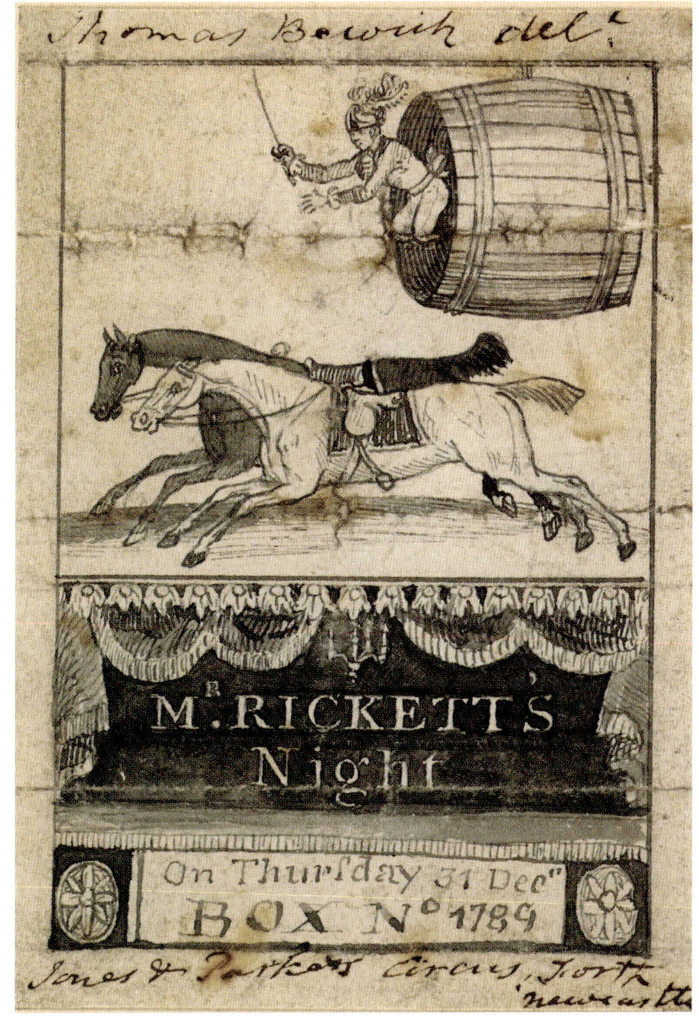

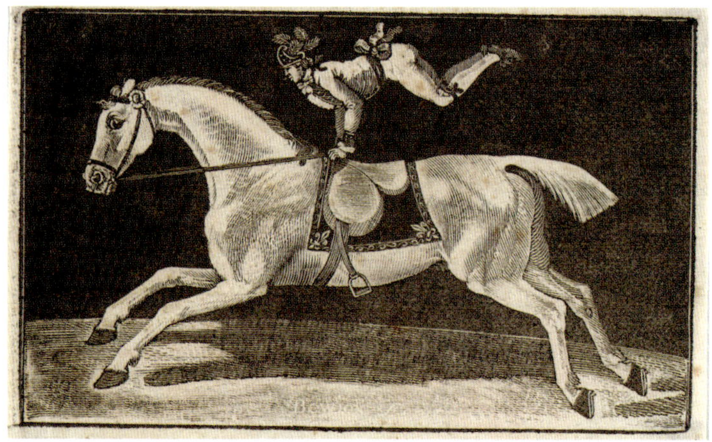

Illustration for a handbill, engraved on wood by Bewick, *c.* 1789, for the circus of Jones and Parker. The performers were famous for their 'voltige' acts in which riders vaulted onto their galloping horses and somersaulted off them. 80 × 122 mm. British Museum 1882,0311.4163.

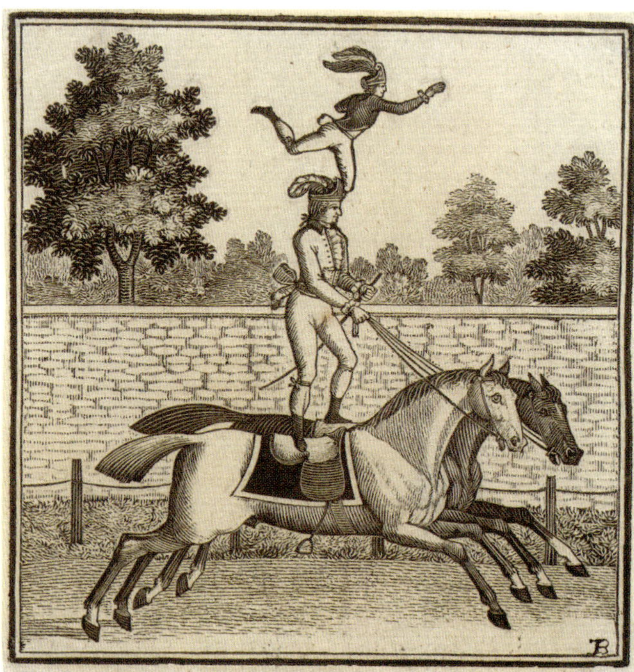

Illustration for a hand or posting bill, engraved on wood by Bewick for Benjamin Handy, 14 July 1792, at a charge of 15s. Handy was a well-known equestrian, whose troupe followed Jones and Parker's at the Forth Circus. Handy's daughter, frequently dubbed 'The Child of Promise' and here shown balancing on his shoulders, often starred in his performances. 115 × 115 mm. British Museum 1882,0311.3183.

Vignette for a benefit night ticket, engraved on wood by Bewick for John Nunn, 16 November 1793, at a charge of 18s. John Nunn and his wife Elizabeth were regular players on the Chester and Newcastle theatrical circuit from 1779. He was described as 'a good low comedian and sang comic songs'. Despite this, and the iconography of pleasures which adorn his benefit night ticket, the play chosen for his benefit, 30 November 1793, was a tragedy, Shakespeare's *Henry VIII*. 80 × 105 mm. British Museum 1882,0311.3220.

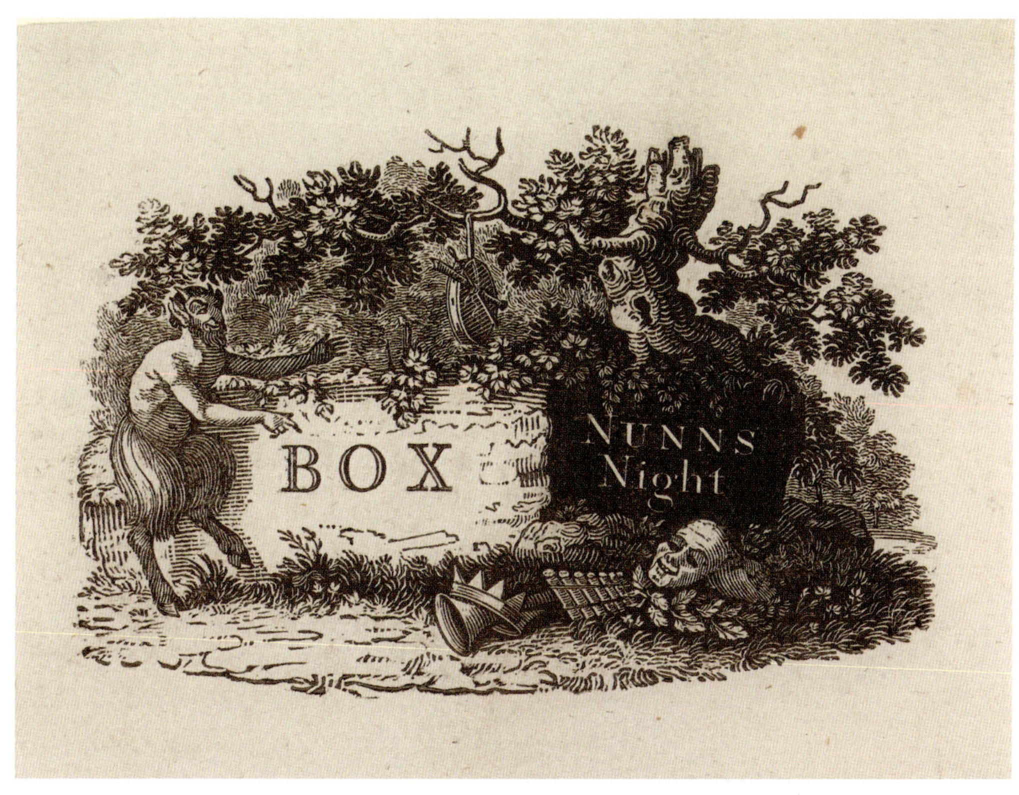

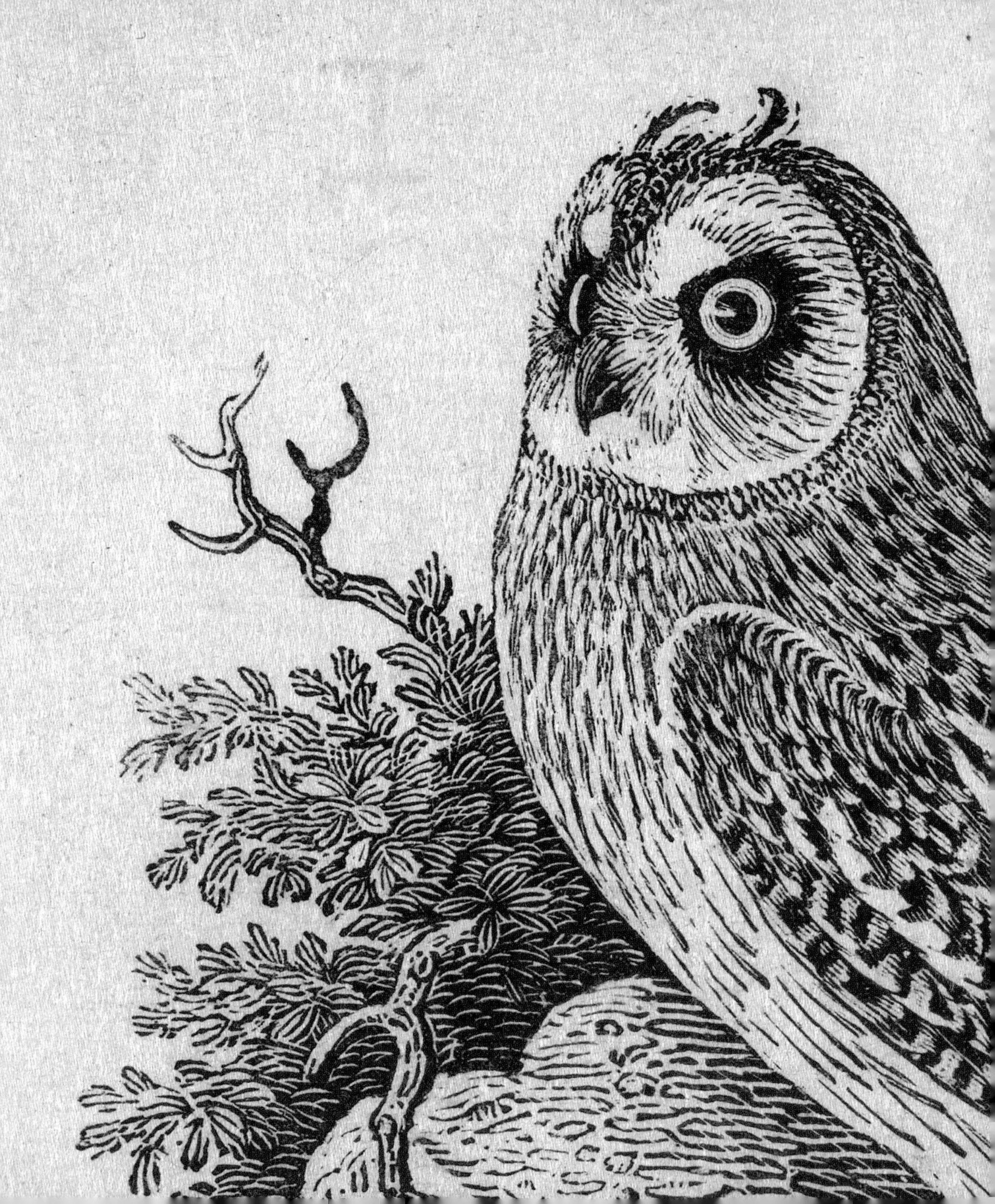

The World of Books and Booklovers

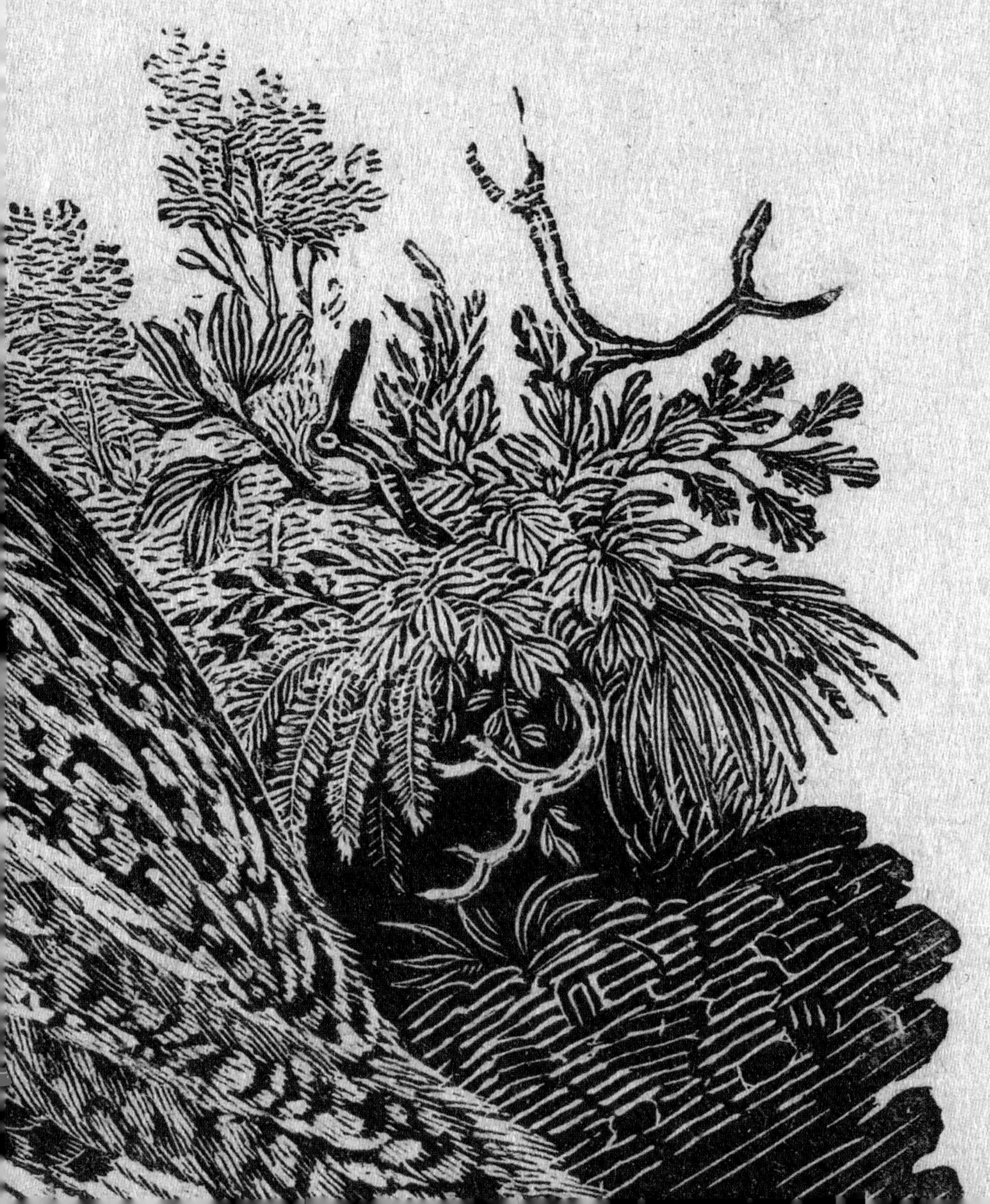

Books

And so to books. Although it was books and their illustrations which brought fame to Bewick in a manner as sudden as it was unsought, this did not occur until publication of his *General History of Quadrupeds* in 1790, twenty-three years after he had first started engraving. Even though Bewick had gained first prize from the Royal Society of Arts early in 1776 for his woodcuts to the forthcoming *Fables by the late Mr Gay*, cutting blocks and engraving copperplates for illustrative purposes was just another branch of jobbing engraving. In addition, since many of the commissions at that time related to mathematical and technical treatises, county histories, surveys and reports, there was precious little room to exercise the imagination

Against all the odds, for it was neither a bookish town nor a centre of learning, Newcastle was home to numerous printers and booksellers who were quick to respond to the changing times. Some printers, like Thomas Saint, were primarily newspapermen. Others, such as Thomas Angus, catered for the enormous appetite for chapbook literature (ballads, romances, histories, myths and legends) amongst the mass of the population, many of whom could read even if they could not write. Carried in their thousands by travelling chapmen, Angus's flimsy productions penetrated deep into the countryside around Newcastle, south as far as York, north beyond the Borders. Some undoubtedly found their way into the farmstead at Cherryburn, and along with a Bible and a Book of Common Prayer, probably made up the sum and total of the literature that furnished Bewick's childhood home.

One trend spotted early by Thomas Saint was the growing recognition amongst the 'middling' classes – and a broad section of the poor – that education was a vital prerequisite for improving a child's lot in life. Saint also perceived how Bewick's talents as both a designer and an engraver on wood could be utilized in illustrating children's books. Here Bewick found an outlet for his imagination. Woodcuts were particularly appropriate for such books, not only because the cuts were generally small in size (branches of boxwood were modest in diameter) and relatively inexpensive compared to copperplates, but also because the blocks sat in the text at the same height as the type and could be printed together, time after time. Children were now courted by booksellers and offered choices, even in the matter of covers; would it be an illustrated cover, 'grown-up' quarter-leather boards, or a spangly, multi-coloured floral paper binding?

Bewick, who adored children, delighted in illustrating these diminutive volumes with their enchanting titles – *The Golden Toy, Fun upon Fun, Pretty Poems for Little Masters and Misses, Mother Chit-Chat's Tales for Youth, Cottage Tales for Little People, The Sugar Plum, The Valentine's Gift* – and perhaps by doing so, compensated a little for his own book-deprived childhood. The duty of care he felt he owed his little readers was sharpened by the memory of his acute dismay when, a child himself, he had eagerly opened a schoolroom copy of *A Description of over Three Hundred Animals* only to find he could barely recognize a single beast or bird amidst the slovenly stamps that passed as illustrations. So keenly did this rankle that he swore then and there that he could – indeed would – do better. This ambition was realized many years later with the *Quadrupeds* in 1790 and the *History of British Birds* in 1797 and 1804.

Chapbook illustration,
engraved on wood by
Bewick, *c.* 1774, for Thomas
Angus. The thief is in the
act of stealing geese; his
destiny is clearly marked by
the gibbet on the horizon, a
moralizing device of which
Bewick never tired.
56 × 75 mm. British
Museum 1882,0311.4574.

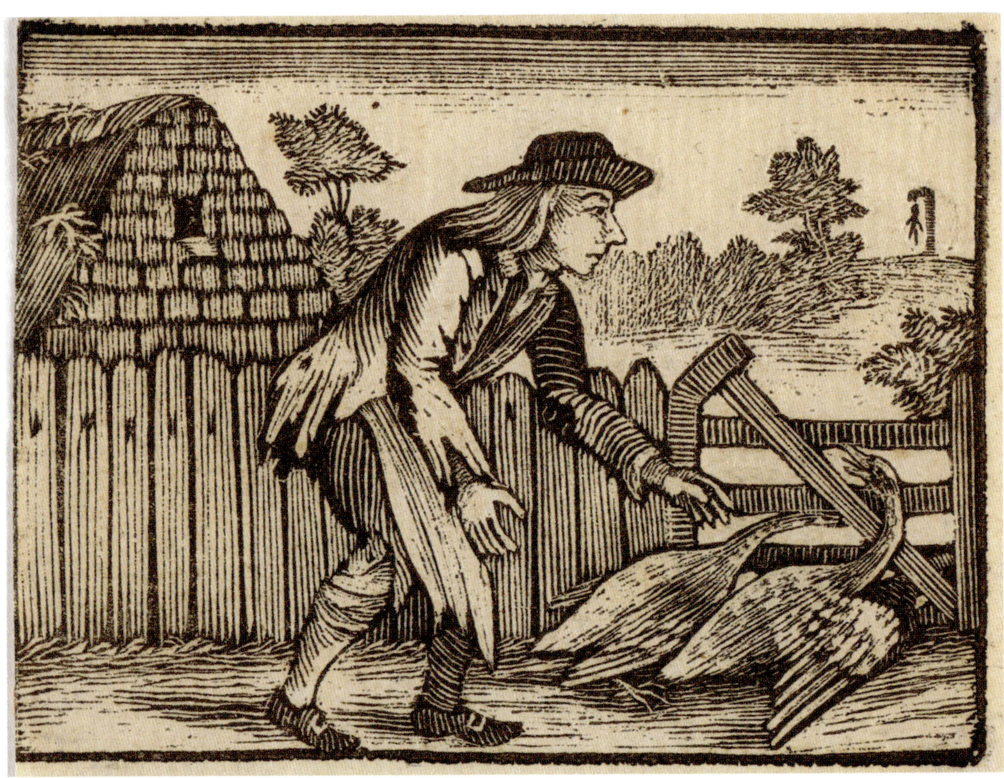

Alphabet cut, engraved on wood by Bewick in 1777, during his stay in London. As the building blocks of literacy, such cuts were in constant demand. They occasionally figure as frontispieces to primers, but many were printed as single leaves. 120 × 70 mm. British Museum 1882,0311.3186.

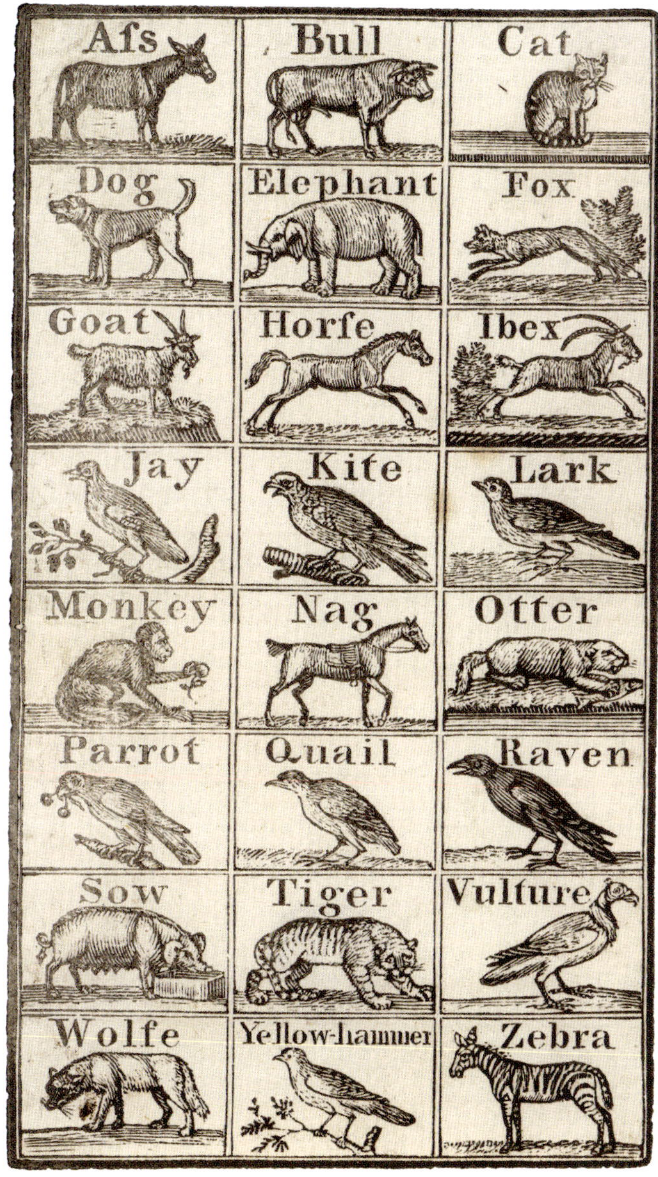

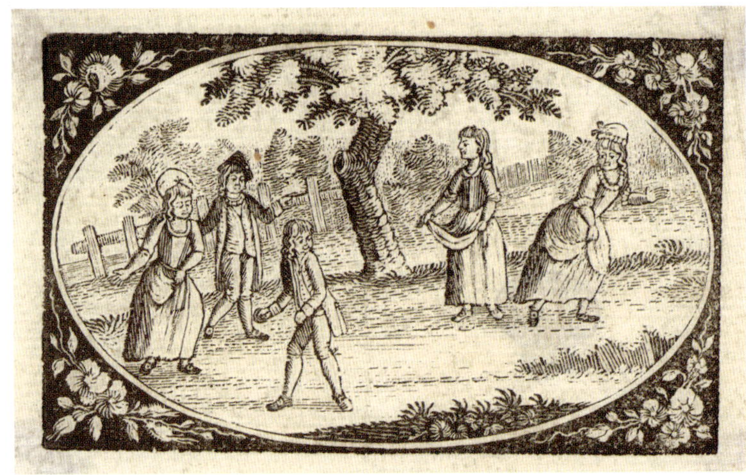

Book cover, engraved on wood by Bewick, *c.* 1777 for Thomas Angus. The girl in the centre is looking for a candidate to start a game of 'blind man's buff'. 60 × 92 mm. British Museum 1882,0311.3710.

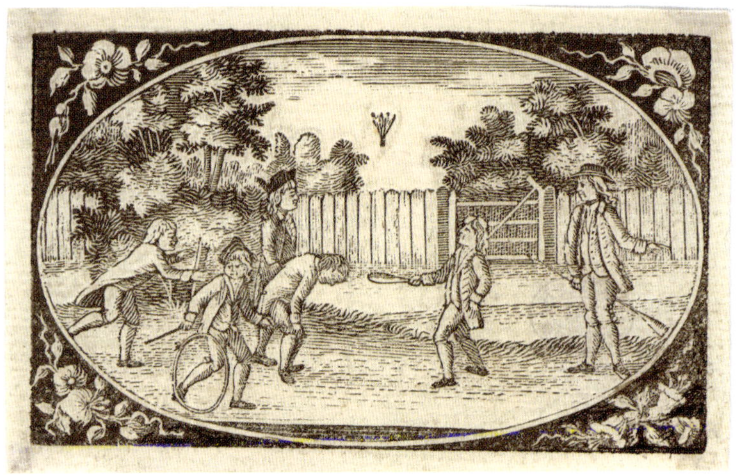

Book cover, engraved on wood by Bewick, *c.* 1777 for Thomas Angus. The boys are depicted playing a variety of games including shuttlecock, bowling a hoop and leapfrog. The older boy on the right appears to be holding a hockey stick. 60 x 92 mm. British Museum 1882,0311.3698.

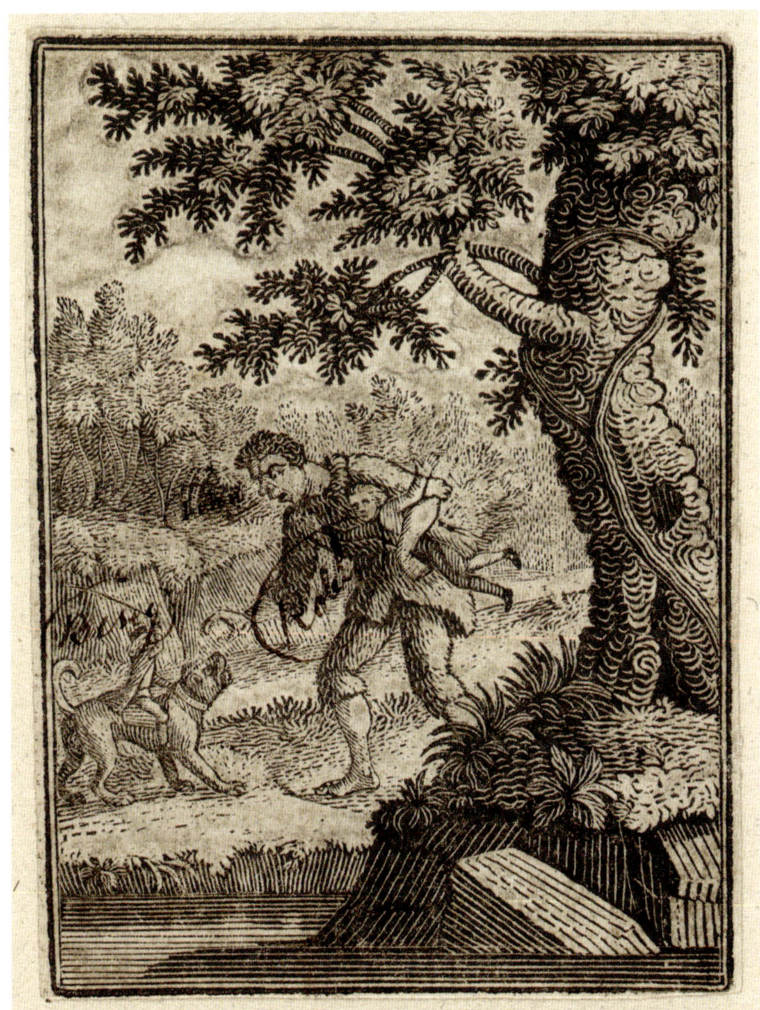

Frontispiece, engraved on wood by Bewick, 1778, at a charge of 15s., for *A Pretty Book of Pictures for Little Masters and Misses*. Two of Bewick's children, Elizabeth and Robert, have shown their appreciation of the engraving by scribbling their names on this proof. 89 × 63 mm. British Museum 1882,0311.2334.

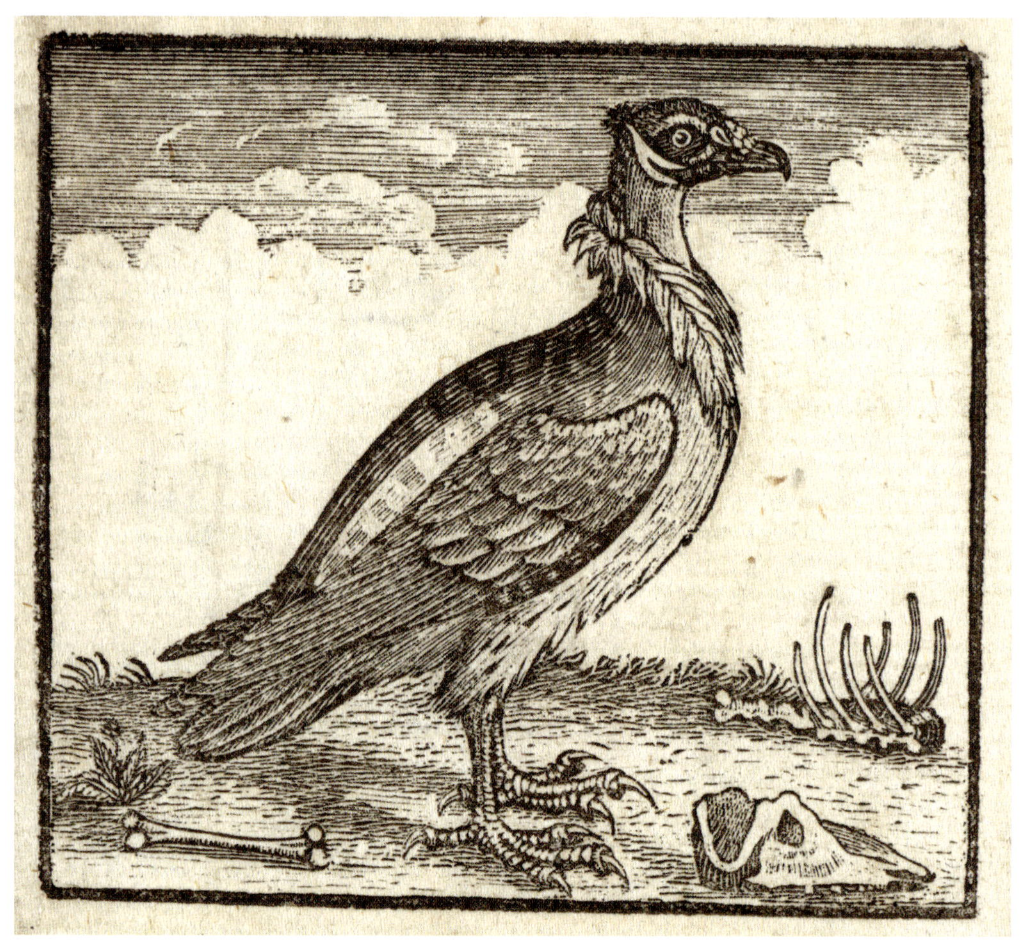

Illustration of a vulture, engraved on wood by Bewick, 1778, at a charge of 5s., for Thomas Saint of Newcastle's edition of *A Pretty Book of Pictures for Little Masters and Misses*, more generally known by its subtitle, *Tommy Trip's History of Beasts and Birds.* This children's book spurred Bewick's intention to compile and edit his renowned natural histories of quadrupeds and birds. 60 × 64 mm. British Museum 1882,0311.2350.

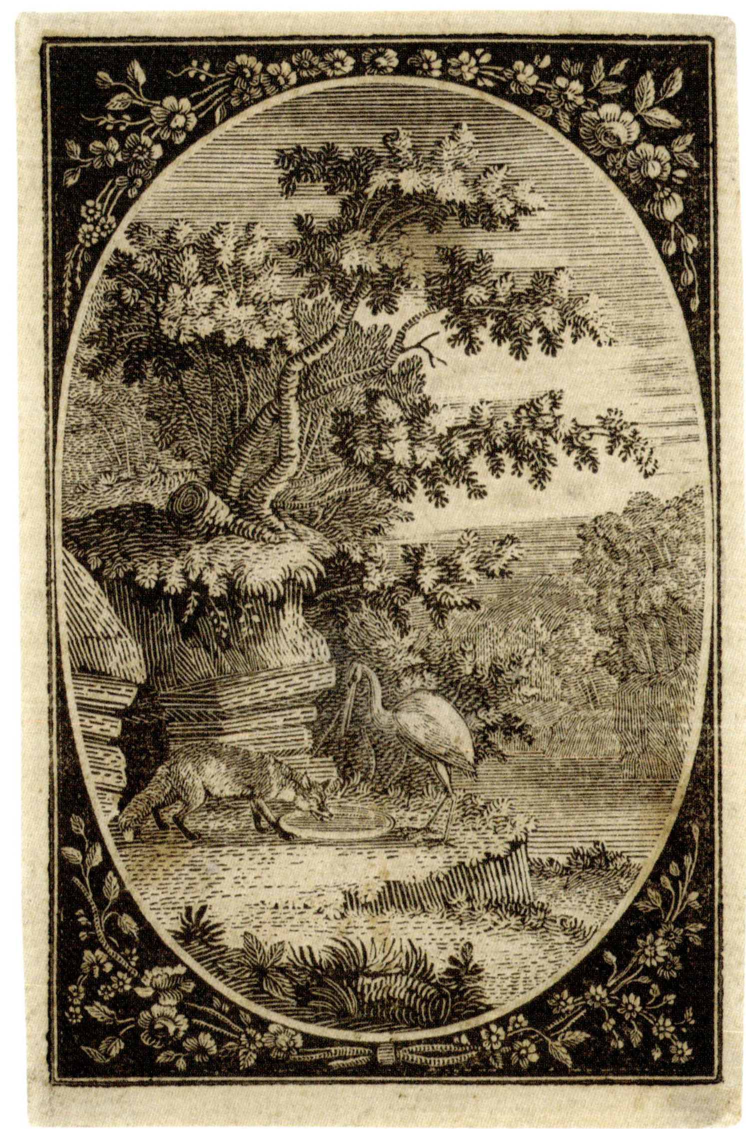

Book cover, engraved on wood by Bewick, *c.* 1779. The engraving illustrates the tale of 'The Fox's Invitation', one of the most popular of Aesop's fables. 107 × 70 mm. British Museum 1882,0311.3696.

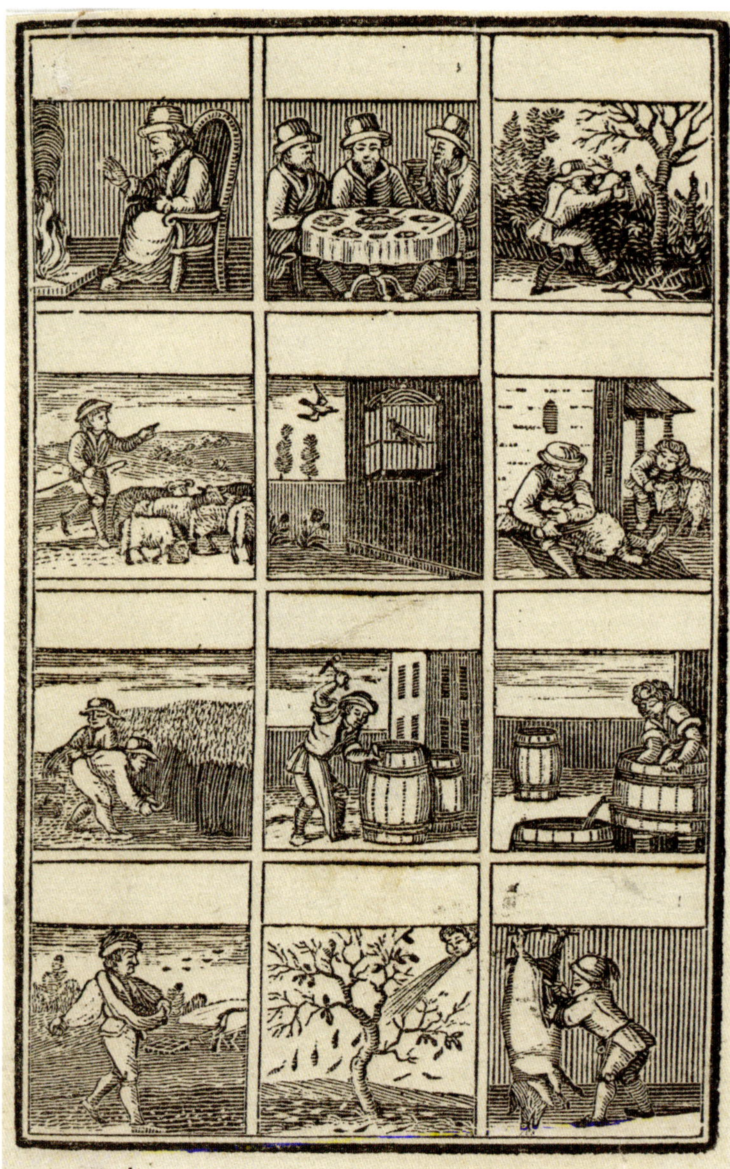

Illustration of the twelve months, engraved on wood by Bewick, *c.* 1780, for a battledore or school exercise; pupils would be required to fill the blanks with the correct month or other facts relevant to the illustrations. 120 × 75 mm. British Museum 1882,0311.3718.

Frontispiece (with hand colouring) engraved on wood by Bewick, 1780, for *Mother Goose's Melody*, showing girls at play and studying. 85 × 75 mm. British Museum 1882,0311.3820.

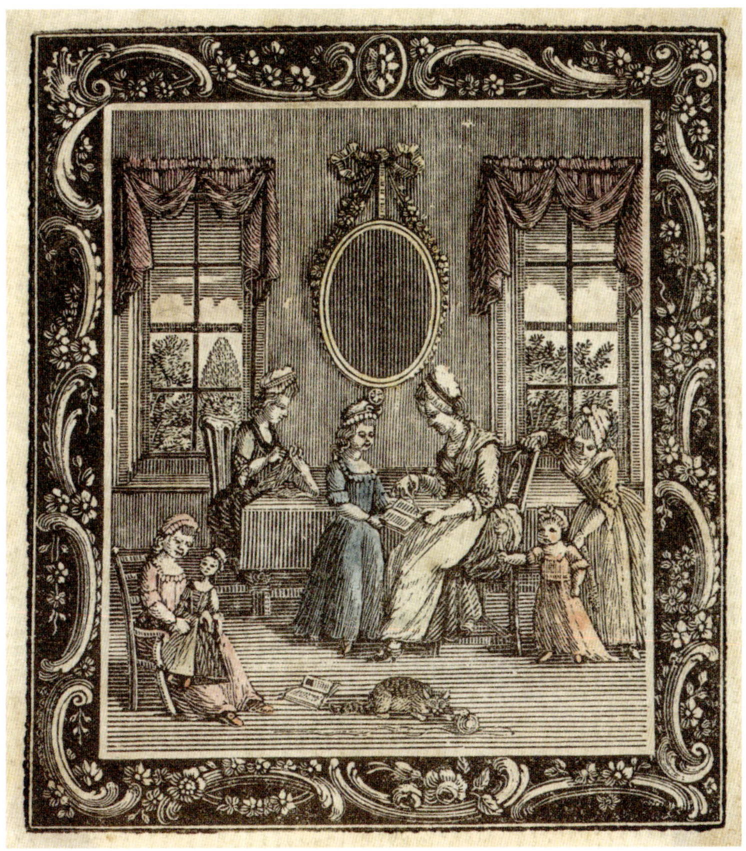

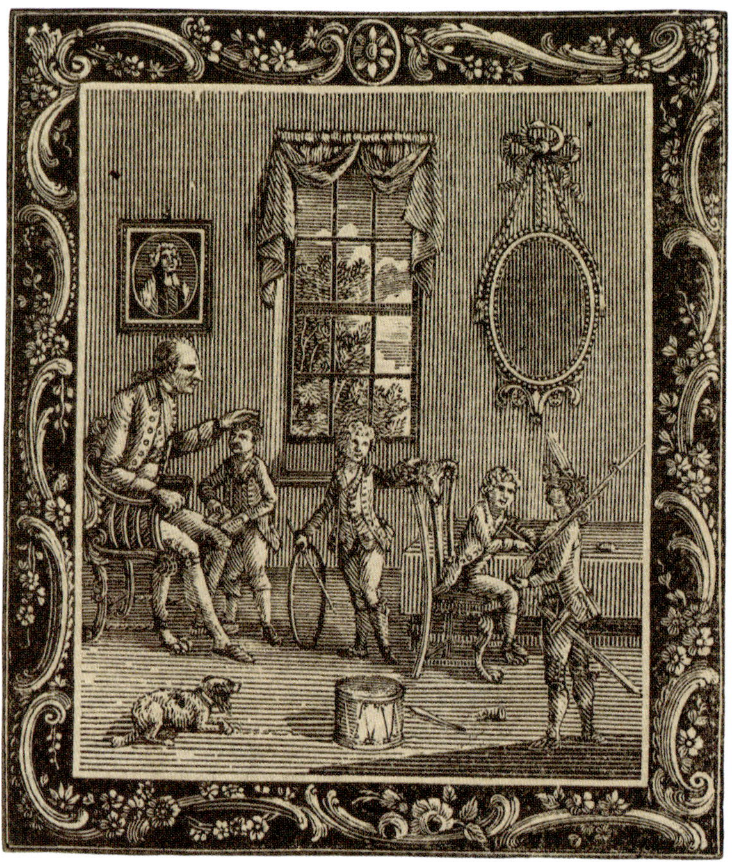

Frontispiece engraved on wood by Bewick, 1780, for *Mother Goose's Melody*, showing boys at play and studying. Both it and the frontispiece shown on the previous page may have been intended as cover illustrations for this most important collection of children's songs (or nursery rhymes as they are termed today). The 'boys at play' did not appear in the published edition but illustrated *A Curious Hieroglyphick Bible* in 1783. 85 × 73 mm. British Museum 1882,0311.3709.

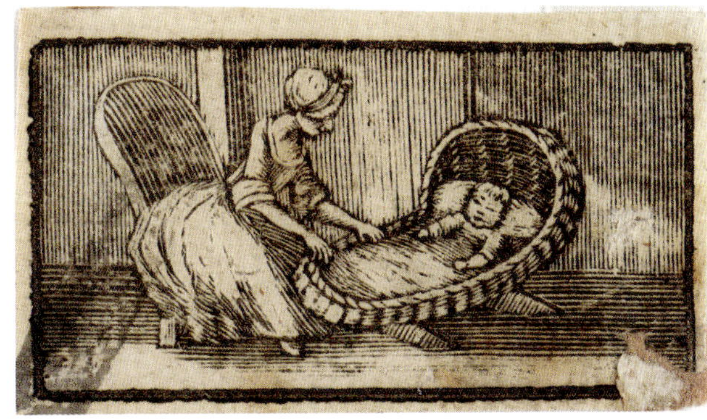

Illustration to 'Hush-a-by-baby', engraved on wood by Bewick, 1780, for *Mother Goose's Melody*. 30 × 52 mm. British Museum 1882,0311.3828.

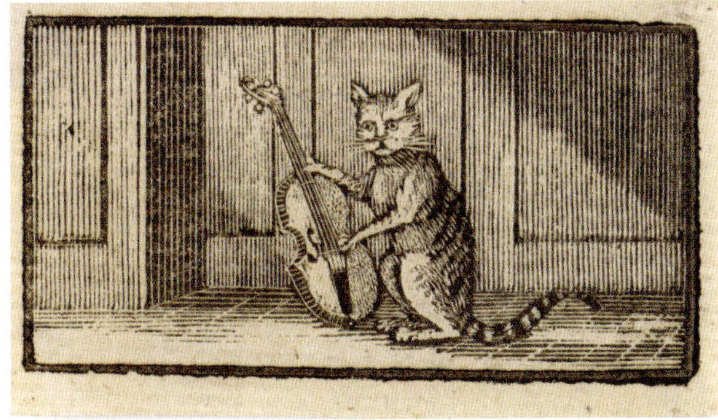

Illustration to 'Hey diddle diddle', engraved on wood by Bewick, 1780, for *Mother Goose's Melody*. 30 × 52 mm. British Museum 1882,0311.3824.

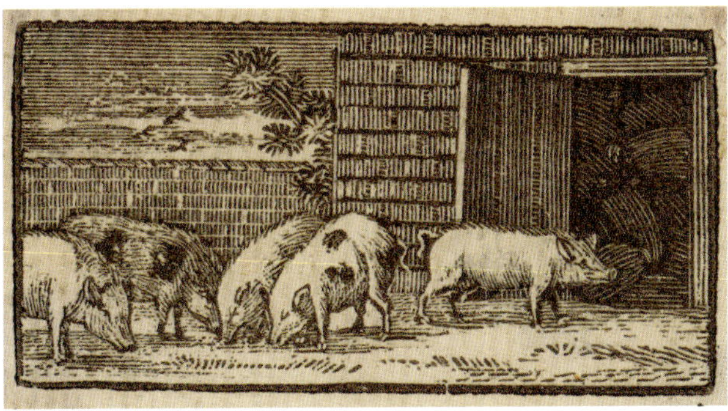

Illustration to 'This little piggy', engraved on wood by Bewick, 1780, for *Mother Goose's Melody*. 30 × 52 mm. British Museum 1882,0311.3841.

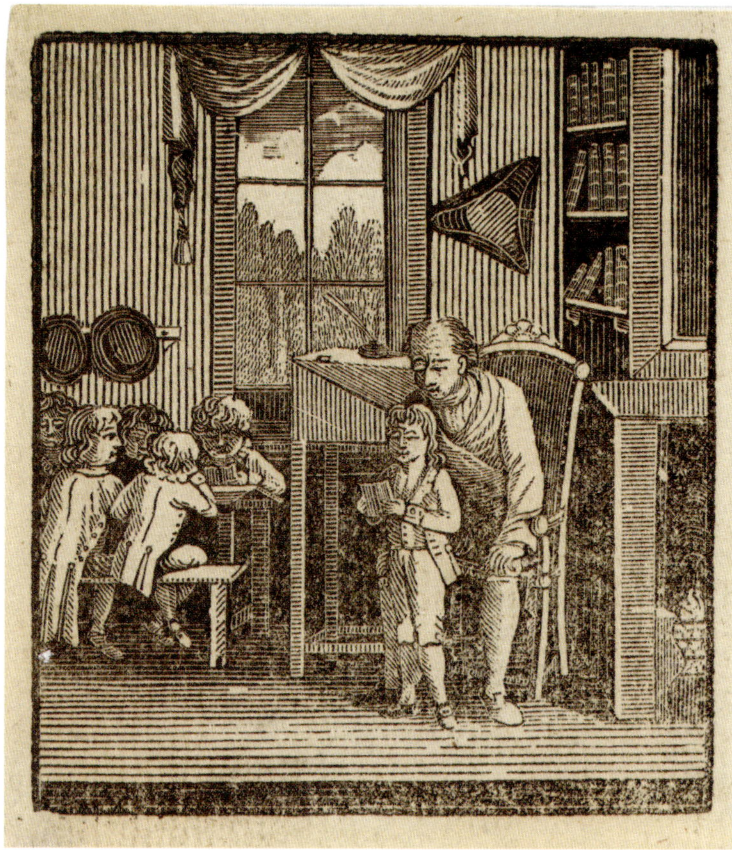

Wood engraving by Bewick, *c.* 1786, for a school book. The boys to the left are revising their books in preparation for the task of reading aloud. The master is more enlightened than most, if the absence of rod or cane is any indication. 75 × 65 mm. British Museum 1882,0311.3794.

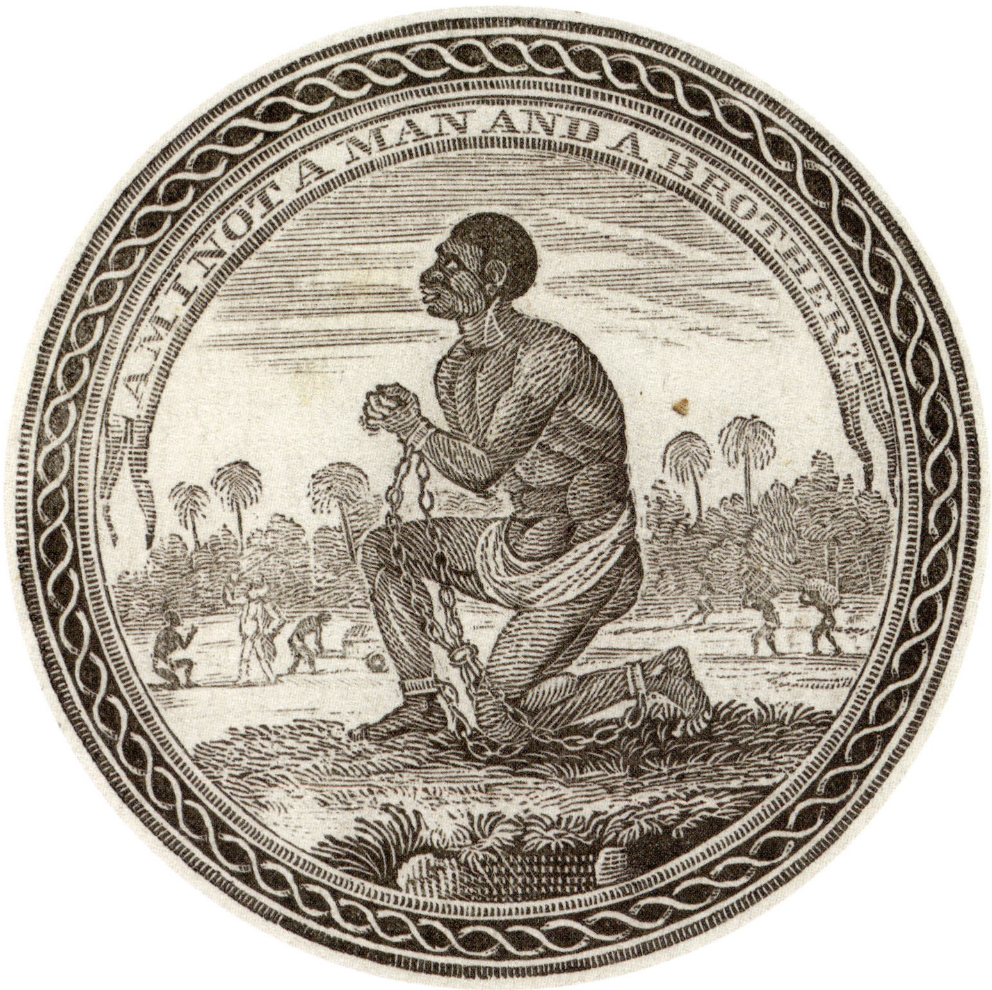

Title-page device, engraved on wood by Bewick,
10 January 1789, at a charge of 15s., for William
Hutchinson's *Princess of Zanfara*. It derives from the
image popularized by Josiah Wedgwood two years
earlier and reflects a sea change in public attitudes
towards the slave trade. 63 mm (diameter).
British Museum 1882,0311.3142.

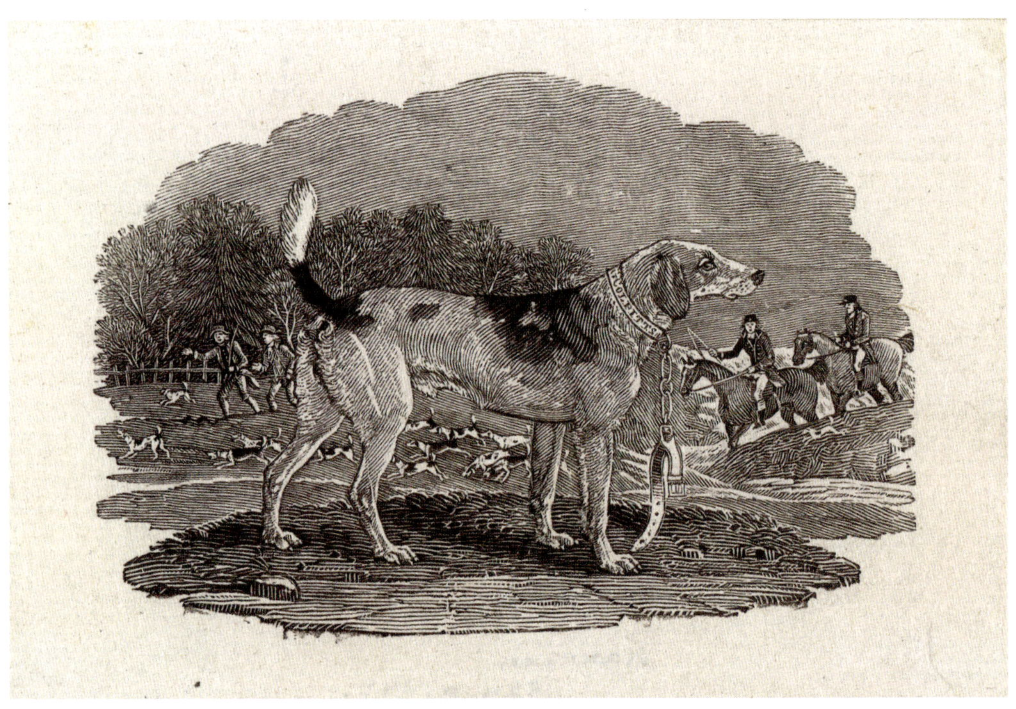

The Harrier, engraved on wood by Bewick for the
General History of Quadrupeds, 1790. On publication
the book met with immediate acclaim and remained
in print for over a quarter of a century, as did his
History of British Birds. 63 × 90 mm. British Museum
1882,0311.2257.

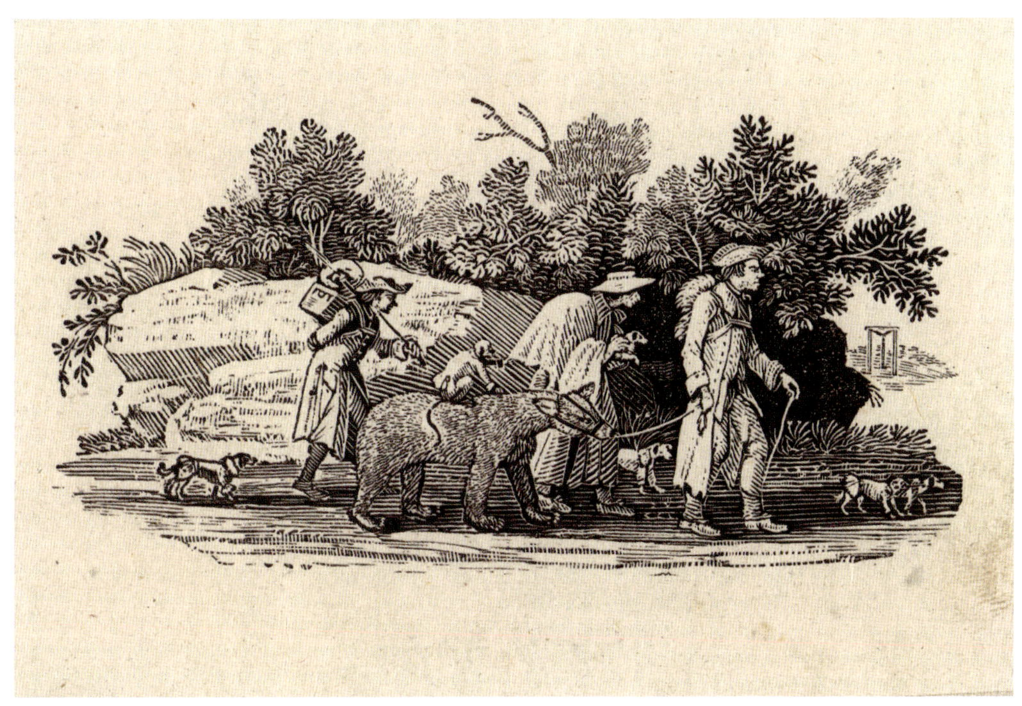

Vignette, engraved on wood by Bewick for the
Quadrupeds, 1790, showing an itinerant showman
and his weary, footsore troupe. The gallows in the
background does not bode well for their future.
Bewick's trenchant 'slice of life' vignettes (which –
as here – often embodied a moralizing intent) were a
revelation, breaking new ground in book illustration.
46 × 85 mm. British Museum 1860.0811.280.

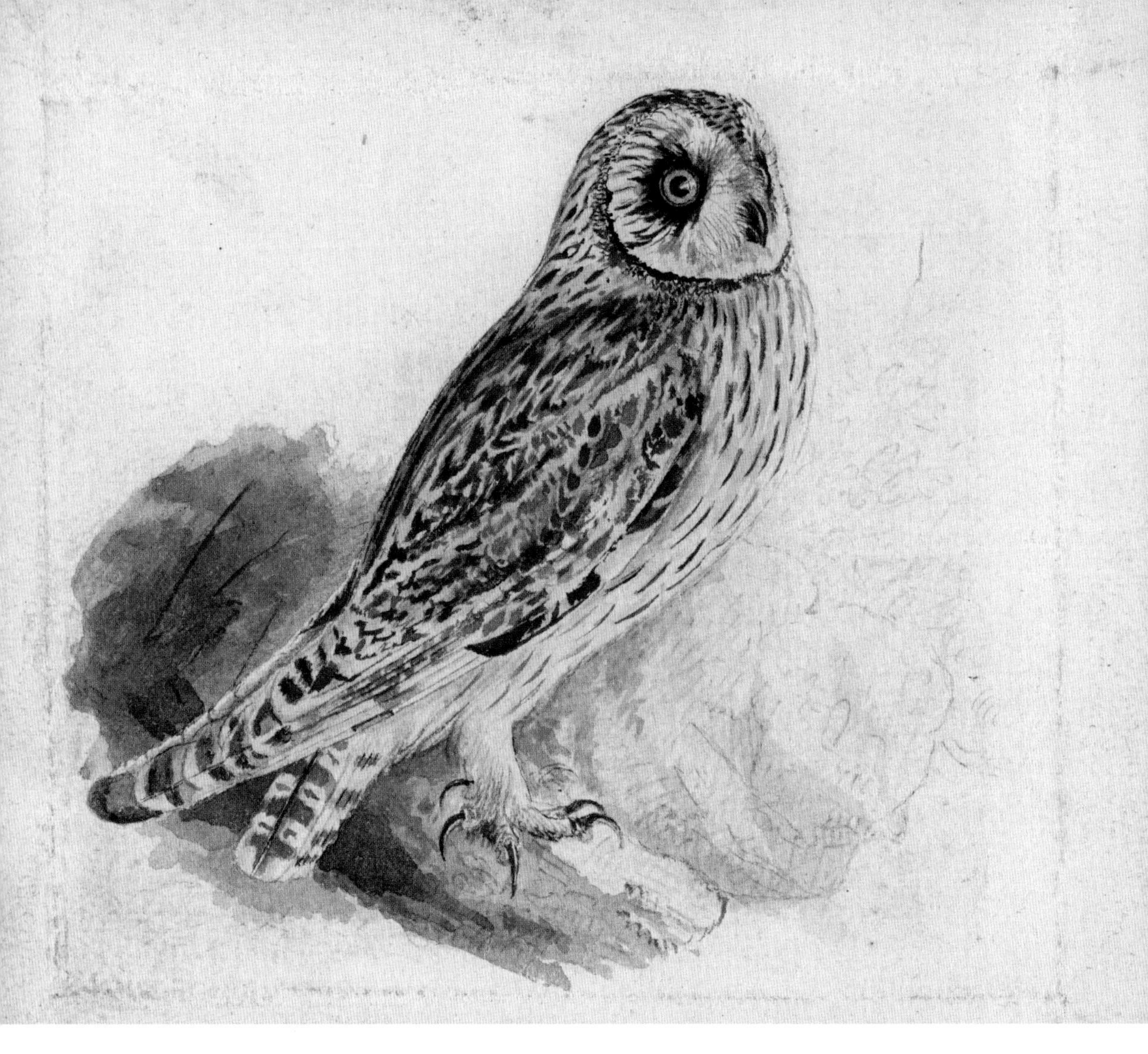

Pen, pencil and
watercolour study by
Bewick of the Short-eared
Owl. 90 × 103 mm. British
Museum 1882,0311.1256.

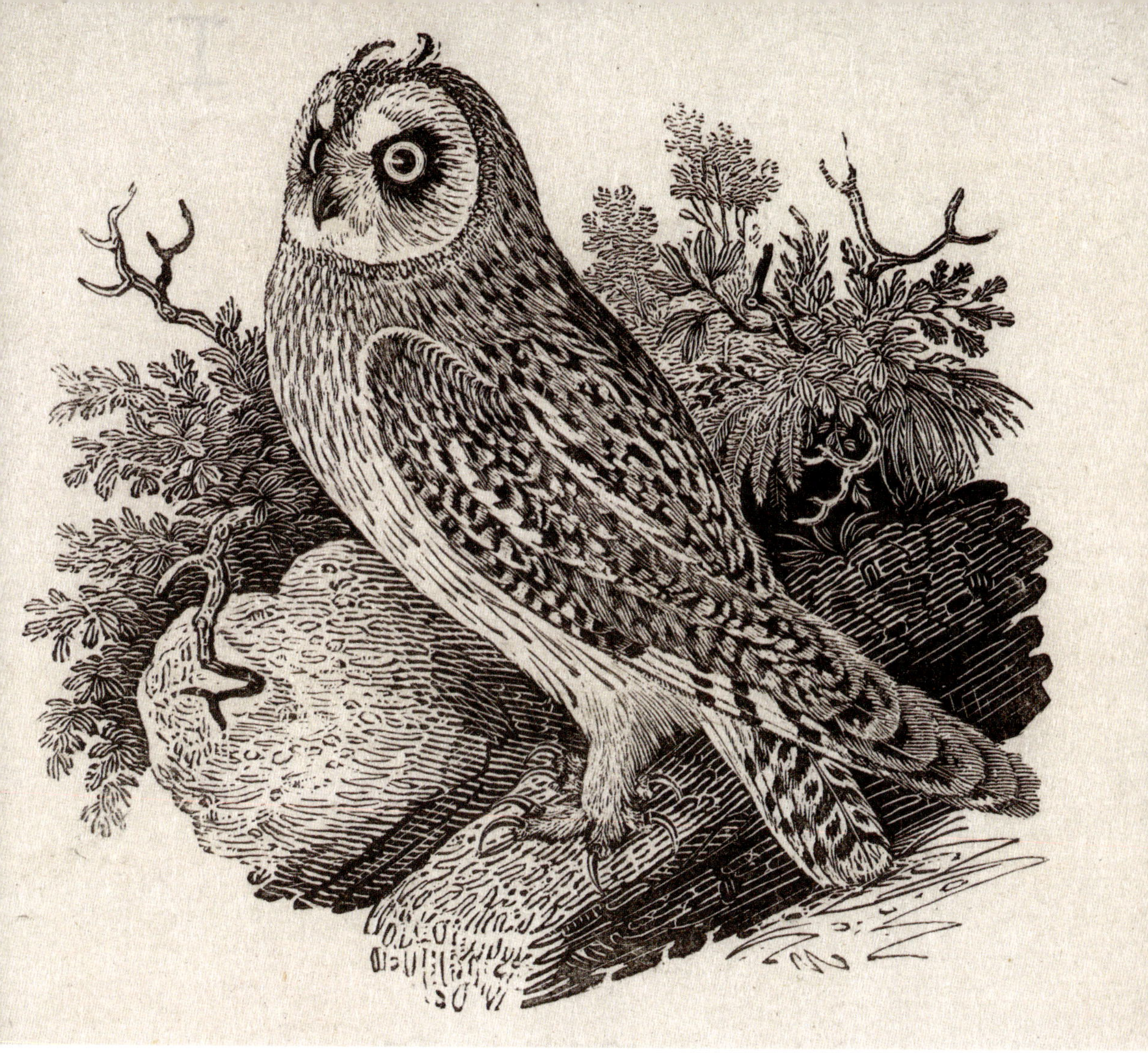

The Short-eared Owl,
engraved on wood by
Bewick for the *Land
Birds*, 1797. 90 × 89 mm.
British Museum 1882,0311.1784.

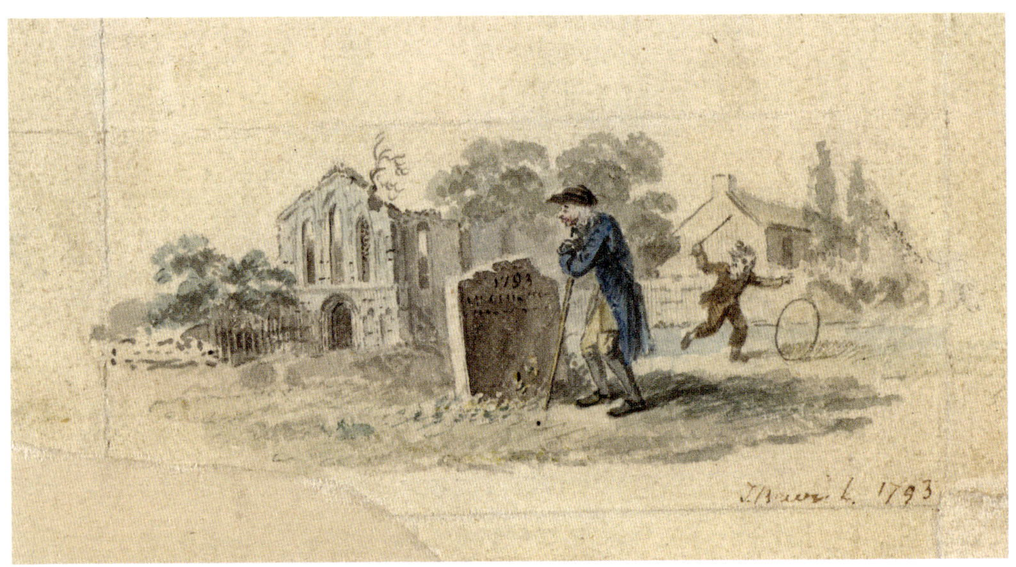

Pencil and watercolour
study by Bewick for
the vignette 'Vanitas
Vantitatum' (a reflection
on the transience of
earthly pursuits).
60 × 95 mm. British
Museum 1882,0311.1344.

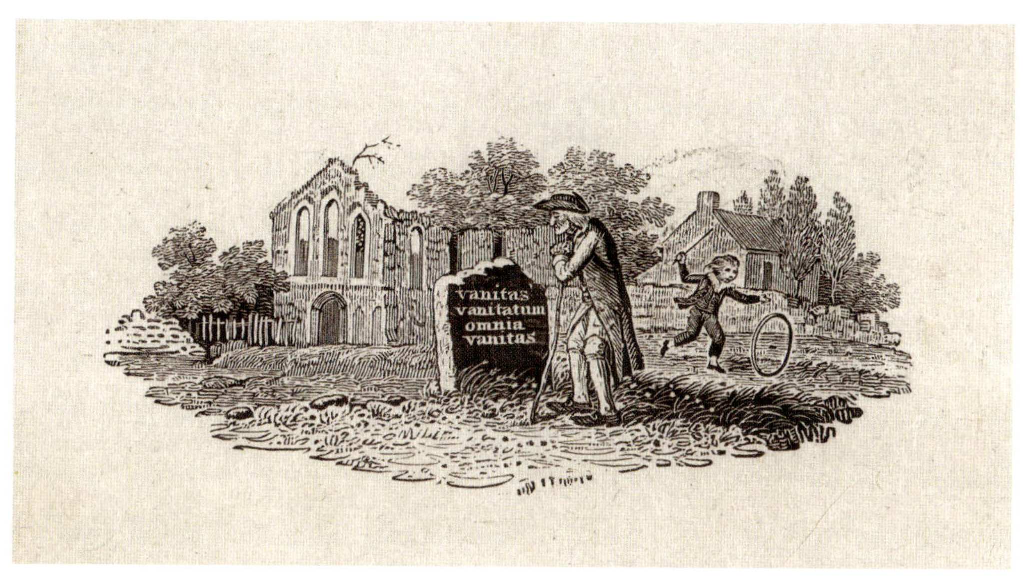

Vignette, 'Vanitas
Vanitatum', engraved on
wood by Bewick for the
Land Birds, 1797.
40 × 85 mm. British
Museum 1860,0811.348.

Pen and watercolour study
by Bewick of the Redshank.
85 × 105 mm. British Museum
1882,0311.1300.

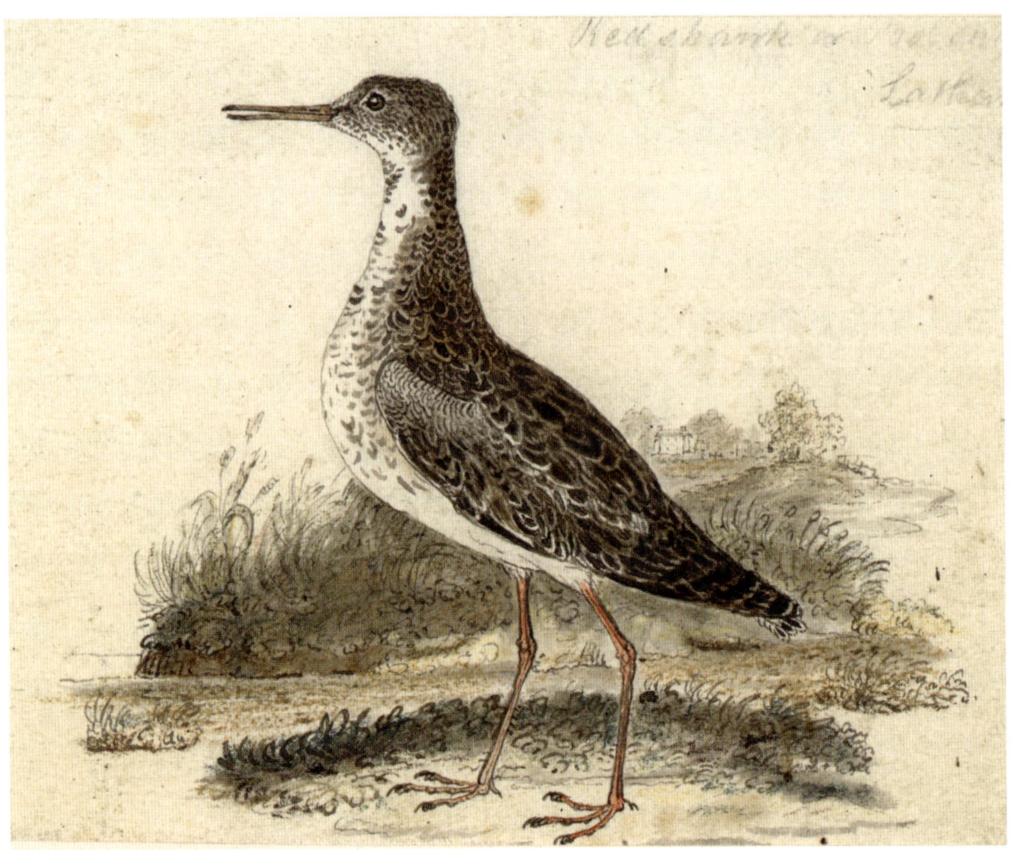

The Redshank, engraved on wood by Bewick, 8 August
1801, for the *Water Birds*, 1804. As usual, the woodcut
incorporates greater vitality and detail than the drawing.
60 × 90 mm. British Museum 1882,0311.1880.

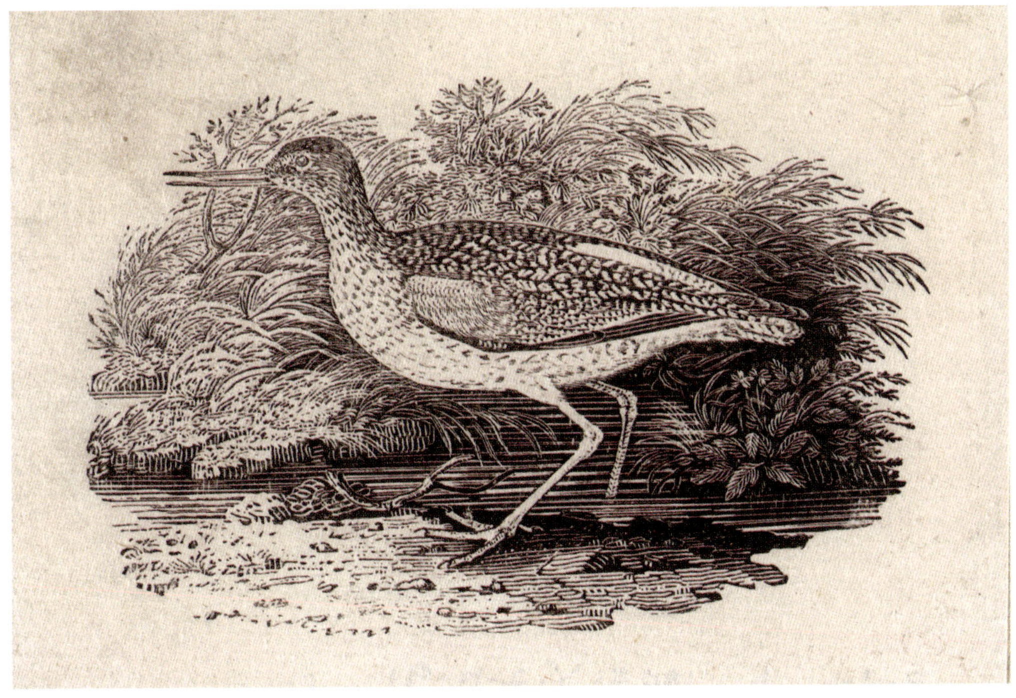

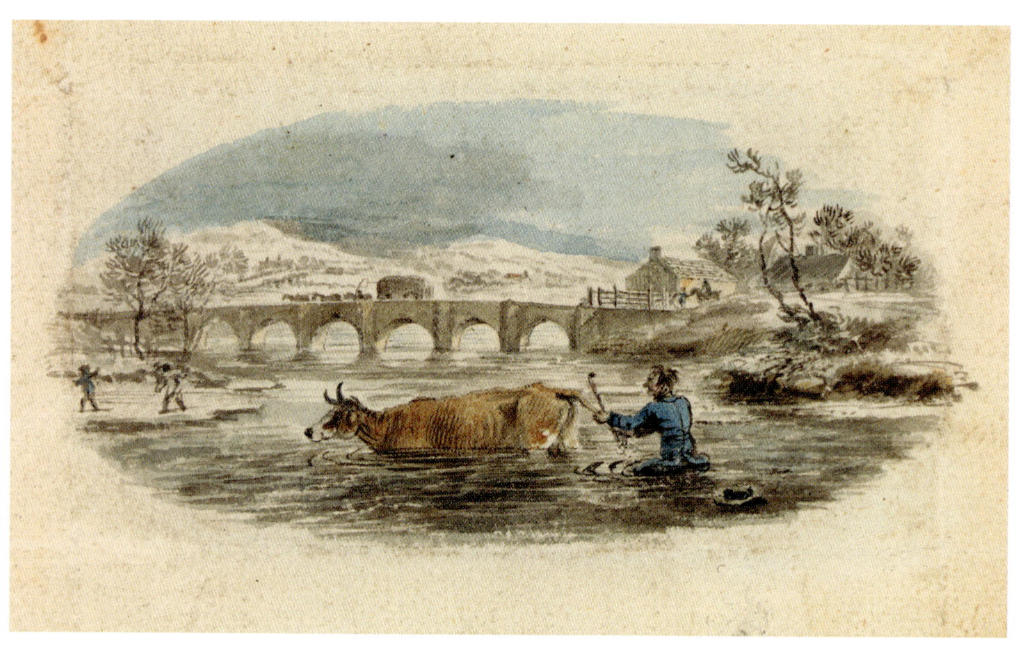

Pencil and watercolour study by Bewick for the
vignette 'Saving the Toll'. 70 × 110 mm.
British Museum 1882,0311.1362.

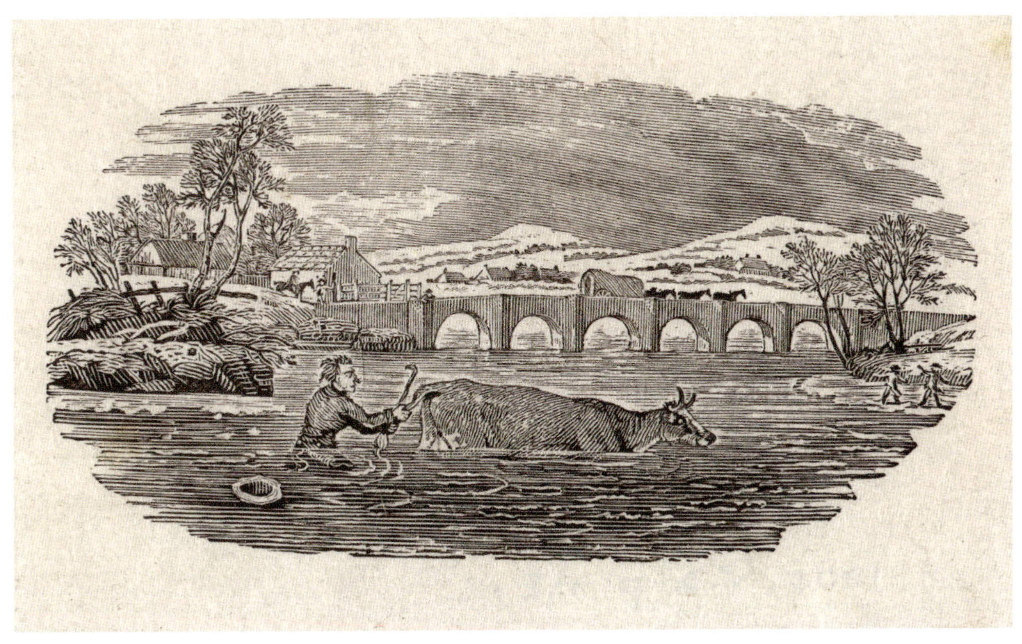

Vignette, 'Saving the Toll', engraved on wood by
Bewick, 23 June 1798, for the *Water Birds*. The
parsimonious farmer, unwilling to pay the toll of a few
pennies to cross the bridge, has elected for the false
economy of braving the icy waters of the wintry Tyne
and has lost his hat into the bargain. 52 × 90 mm.
British Museum 1882,0311.1995.

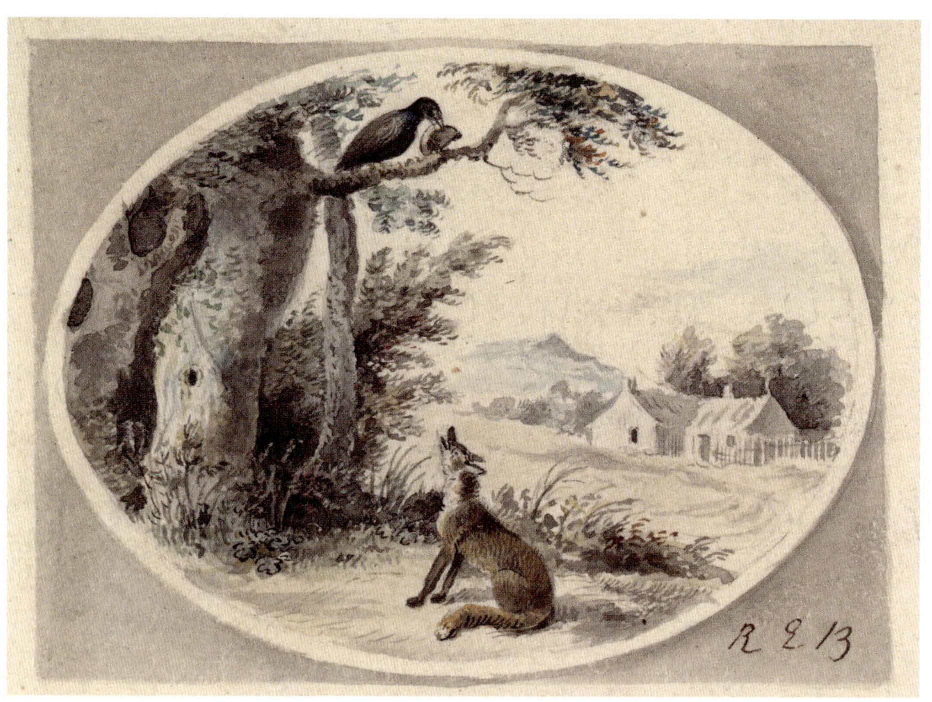

Pencil and watercolour study by Bewick – or possibly
by Robert Elliot Bewick (R E B) – for the fable of
'The Fox and the Crow'. 53 × 70 mm. British Museum
1882,0311.1607.

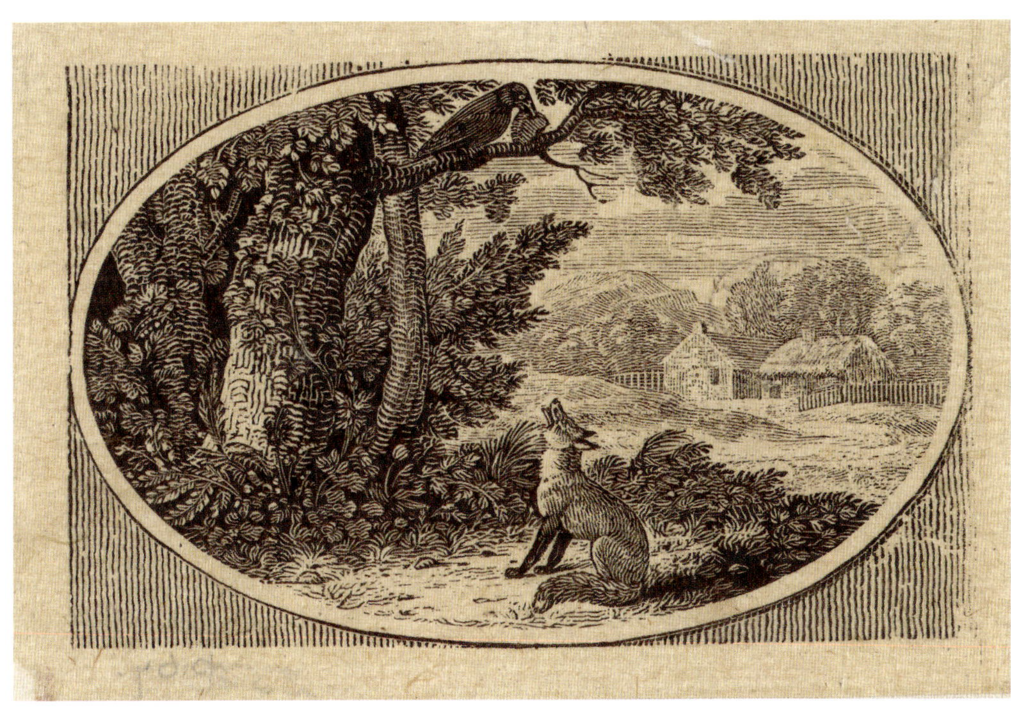

'The Fox and the Crow', engraved on wood by Bewick(?) for the *Fables of Aesop*, 1818. Commenced about 1811, progress on the *Fables* was interrupted by bouts of ill-health and slowed by Bewick's declining powers. His best apprentices were drafted in to assist but on publication the book was perceived as old-fashioned and public acclaim was muted. 55 × 80 mm. British Museum 1882,0311.2432.

Bookplates

In the eighteenth century, gentlemen (and a few gentle ladies) expected to insert bookplates into the volumes in their libraries, and commissions for engraving and printing them figured early in Ralph Beilby's career. Engraved on copper and featuring an armorial device and motto, they were predictable, greatly to Beilby's taste and suited his capabilities perfectly. However, the rise of a wealthy 'middling' class, tradesmen and merchants with substantial libraries but with no right to a coat of arms, changed everything. As luck would have it, the pictorial bookplate came into fashion at about the same time as the reading public applauded Bewick's woodcut vignettes to his *Quadrupeds* and the art of the bookplate, largely moribund until then, gained immeasurably thereby.

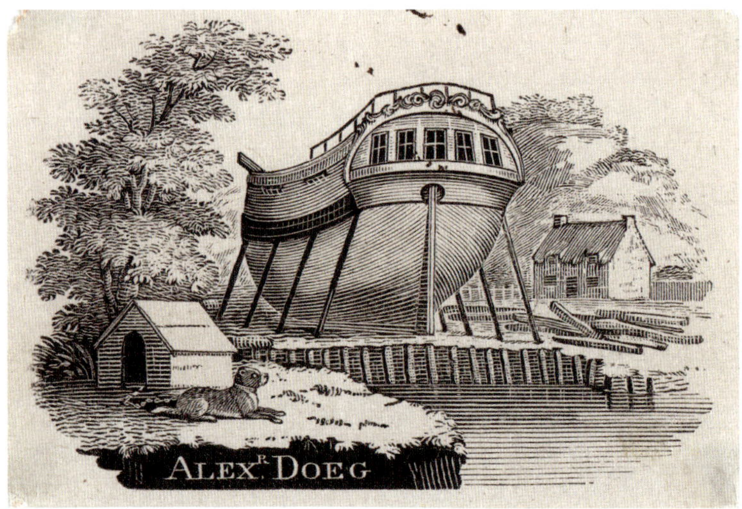

Bookplate for Alexander Doeg, shipwright of Gateshead, engraved on wood by Bewick, 22 April 1792, at a charge of 10s. 6d. The scene shows Doeg's slipway on the Tyne. 54 × 90 mm. British Museum 1882,0311.3650.

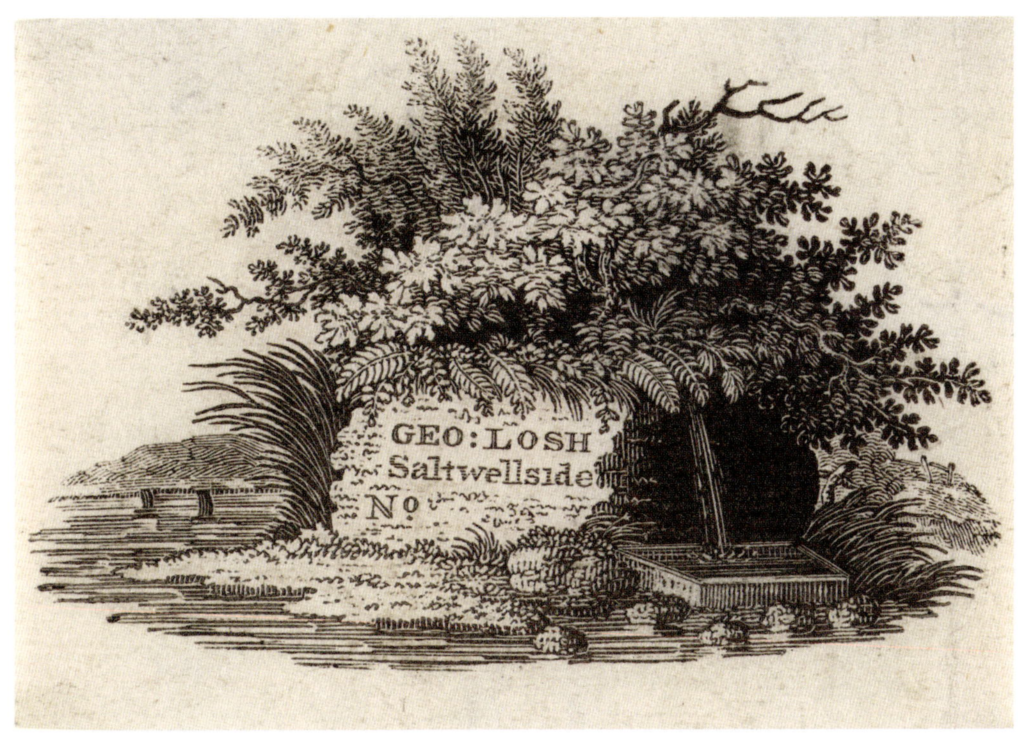

Bookplate for George Losh, merchant and industrialist of Newcastle, engraved on wood by Bewick, 10 May 1800, at a charge of £1 1s. 0d. 60 × 85 mm. British Museum 1882,0311.3239.

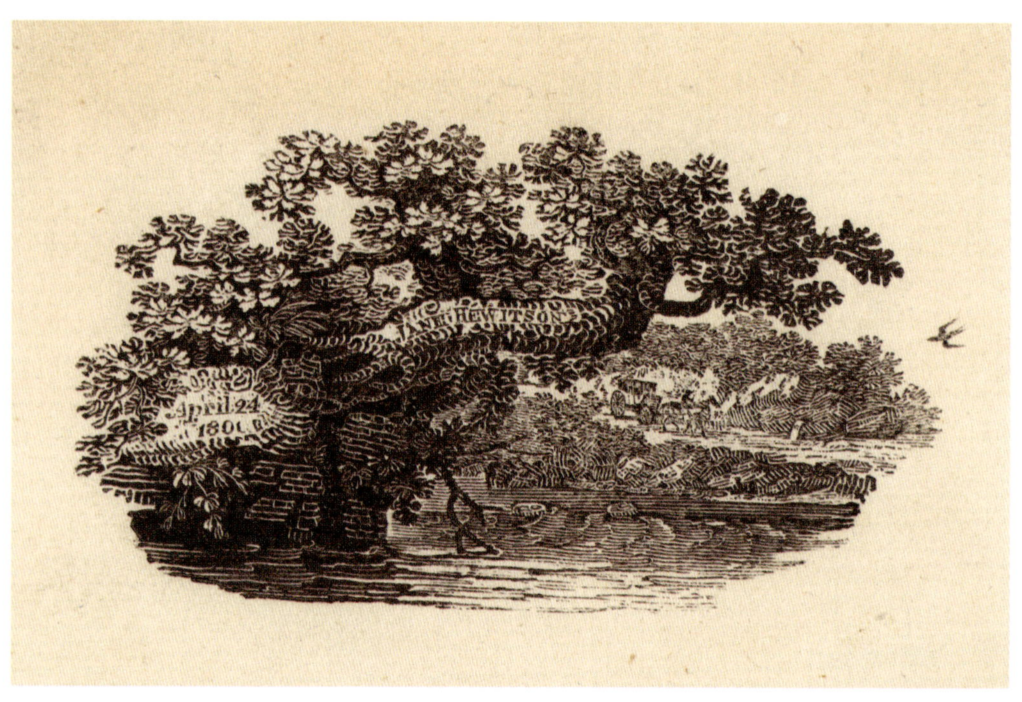

Bookplate for Jane
Hewitson, wife of
Middleton Hewitson,
lead merchant and bottle
manufacturer. Newcastle,
engraved on wood by
Bewick, 22 May 1801,
at a charge of 18s.
50 × 85 mm. British
Museum 1848,0809.17.

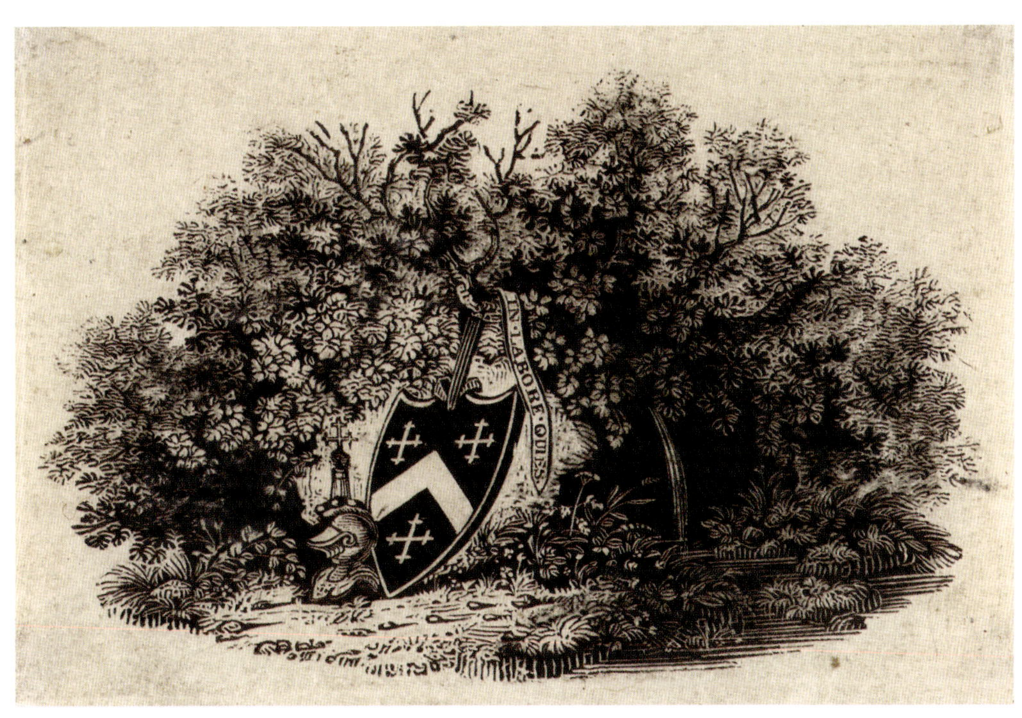

Bookplate for Robert
Southey, poet laureate,
engraved on wood by
Bewick, 7 August 1813,
at a charge of £2 12s. 6d.
Southey had no right
to the arms displayed.
56 × 85 mm. British
Museum 1882,0311.3676.

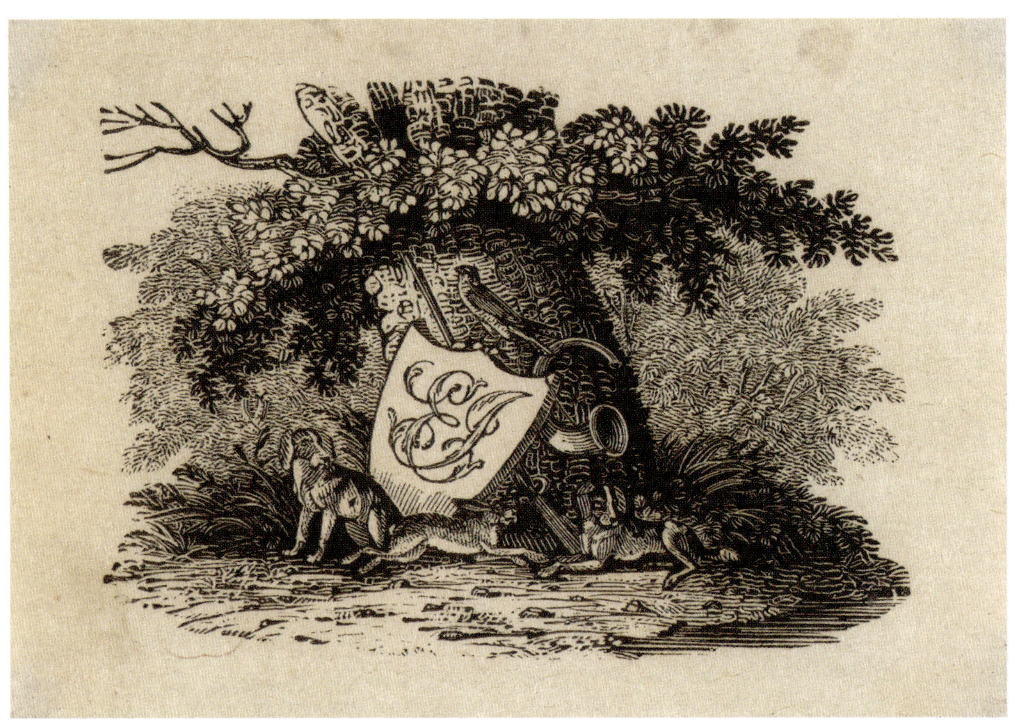

Bookplate for Edmund Jenney, landowner of Hasketon, Suffolk, engraved on wood by Bewick, 22 January 1814, at a charge of £1 11s. 6d. The device reflects Jenney's passion for hunting. 61 × 85 mm. British Museum 1882,0311.3666.

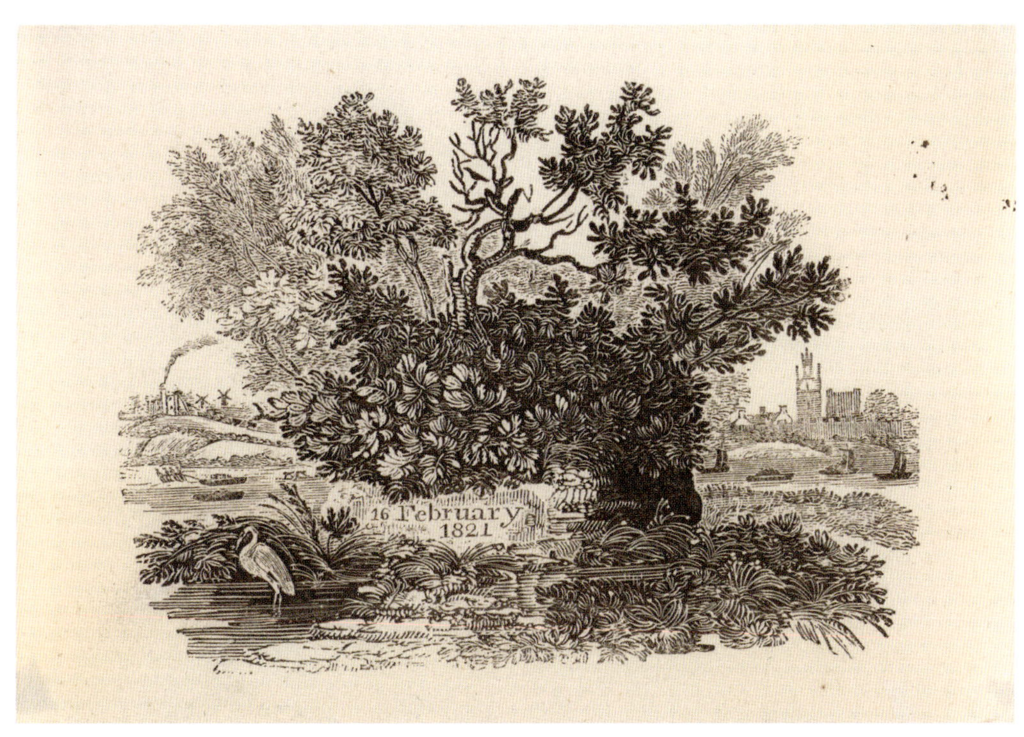

Bookplate for Barbara Liddell of North Shields,
engraved on wood by Bewick, 4 March 1822, at a charge
of £3 13s. 6d. Nature reigns supreme in the foreground,
but beyond lies industrial Tyneside in all its variety:
smoky chimneys, windmills and keels to the left, keels
and colliers to the right, with the battlemented walls
of the town, St Nicholas Church spire and the castle
keep in the distance. 81 × 110 mm. British Museum
1882,0311.3667.

The World of Books and Booklovers **139**

Acknowledgements

This book grew out of a small exhibition of Thomas Bewick's work, held in the public gallery of the British Museum's Department of Prints and Drawings during December 2011 and January 2012 at the suggestion of Sheila O'Connell, one of the Department's Assistant Keepers. The author would like to thank her for her help and encouragement during the writing of this book and to acknowledge the invaluable assistance provided by Iain Bain (the doyen of Bewick authorities), Hugo Chapman (Keeper of Prints and Drawings at the British Museum), Kirstin Kennedy and Rebecca Wallis (curators at the Victoria and Albert Museum), June Holmes of the Natural History Society of Northumbria, and Rosemary Bradley and Alice White of the British Museum Press.

Editorial notes

Wherever dates of engravings are cited in descriptions, these refer to week-ending dates, not to the precise day the engravings were executed. The archive entries usually indicate the cost of each engraving; these are in pre-decimalized sterling of pounds, shillings and pence. Pounds remain the same, but in the old days there were 12 pennies to a shilling (one shilling was roughly equivalent to 5p today) and 20 shillings to a pound.

Graphic sources

Unless otherwise stated, all images in this book derive from the collection held at the Department of Prints and Drawings of the British Museum and are © The Trustees of the British Museum.

In 1882, Bewick's daughter Isabella gave the British Museum more than 4,000 drawings and proofs of prints by her father, his brother John and his son Robert Elliot Bewick. Illustrations from this gift are identified in the captions by registration numbers beginning 1882,0311. The works themselves can be viewed without prior appointment by visiting the Prints and Drawings Study Room and digitally via Collection Online on the British Museum website: britishmuseum.org/collection.

Manuscript sources

Tyne and Wear Archive Services, Newcastle upon Tyne, financial records of the workshop of Ralph Beilby, Thomas Bewick and Robert Bewick, 1751–1882.

Published sources

Berg, Maxine. *Luxury and Pleasure in Eighteenth Century Britain.* Oxford, 2005

Berg, Maxine and Elizabeth Eger (editors). *Luxury in the Eighteenth Century: Debates, Desires and Delectable Goods.* Basingstoke, 2003

Bermingham, Ann and John Brewer (editors). *The Consumption of Culture 1600–1800.* London, 1995

Berry, H. 'Polite consumption', *Transactions of the Royal Historical Society,* 12, 2002

Brewer, John. *Pleasures of the Imagination: English Culture in the Eighteenth Century.* New York, 1997

Brewer, John and Roy Porter (editors). *Consumption and the World of Goods.* London, 1993

Ellison, Margaret. 'The Tyne glasshouses and the Beilby and Bewick workshop', *Archæologia Aeliana,* fifth series, vol. III, 1975

Gill, M. A. V. 'Potteries of Tyne and Wear and their dealings with the Ralph Beilby/ Thomas Bewick workshop', *Archæologia Aeliana,* fifth series, vol. IV, 1976

McKendrick, Neil, John Brewer and John Harold Plumb. *The Birth of a Consumer Society: the Commercialisation of Eighteenth Century England.* London, 1983

Rickards, Maurice. *The Encyclopedia of Ephemera: a Guide to the Fragmentary Documents of Everyday Life.* London, 2000

Voth, Hans-Joachim. 'Time and Work in Eighteenth-Century London', *University of Oxford, Discussion Papers in Economics and Social History,* 21, December 1997

Williams-Wood, Cyril. *English Transfer-Printed Pottery and Porcelain: a History of Over-glaze Printing.* London, 1981

Suggestions for further reading

Bain, Iain. *Thomas Bewick: an Illustrated Record of his Life and Work.* Newcastle, 1979

Bain, Iain. *The Watercolours and Drawings of Thomas Bewick and his Workshop Apprentices.* 2 vols. London, 1981

Bewick, Thomas. *A Memoir ... written by himself.* Edited with an introduction by Iain Bain. London, 1975

Roscoe, Sydney. *Thomas Bewick: a Bibliography Raisonné.* Oxford, 1953

Tattersfield, Nigel. *Bookplates by Beilby & Bewick.* London, 1999

Tattersfield, Nigel. *Thomas Bewick: the Complete Illustrative Work.* 3 vols. 2011

Uglow, Jenny. *Nature's Engraver: a Life of Thomas Bewick.* 2006